CREEPING BLACK MOLD

Dr. Gene Schuyler

CREEPING BLACK MOLD!
Published by Rebecca Publications

Copyright © 2016 by Gene Schuyler
First Printing 2016
ISBN: 978-0-9908873-1-7

Cover design by: Marie Schuyler

Scripture quotations are from:
The Holy Bible, King James Version (KJV) unless otherwise stated.

Printed in the United States of America

ALL RIGHTS RESERVED
No part of this publication may be reproduced, stored in a retrieval system or transmitted in any form by any means - electronic, mechanical, photocopy, recording or otherwise - without prior permission of the publisher, except as provided by USA copyright law.

For information:
REBECCA PUBLICATIONS
1000 BAKERTOWN ROAD
FUQUAY-VARINA, NC 27526

DEDICATION

In giving these messages to the good people of the Mid-Way Baptist Church in Raleigh, North Carolina, during the Sunday evening services, to them all, thanks. I also dedicate this book to my wonderful wife, Marie, for her dedication and her walk with her Savior as a supportive wife, mother and Bible teacher.

PURPOSE

I had a twofold purpose to teach this series to our church and to publish this book: First, to the unsaved that they may have a clear understanding of what the Bible says about sin and second, to the building up and strengthening of the saved to win the war against the sins listed in Proverbs, chapter six.

"CREEPING BLACK MOLD"

The Seven Sins of Proverbs

Introduction:

"Not only that, the mold, they cover it up before you move in and then the real black, furry, nasty mess comes creeping back. It is terrible."

"There's a monster in the walls, and they don't know how to stop it."

The couple first discovered the black mold spreading in the closet of their son's bedroom, which backs up to a bathroom.

"We cleaned it up and he's been doing well about keeping things out of his closet, but the mold keeps creeping back in," Dad said. He's worried that the mold will multiply into other parts of the home, and that it might be endangering his family's health.

Stac/hy/botrys char/tarum is a particular species of mold in the genus Stac/hy/botrys. It is commonly known as **"black mold"** or **"toxic black mold."** When first viewing, it can indeed seem unnerving. It looks as if large black spots interspersed with gray areas have suddenly started appearing on surfaces. Black mold has been linked to health problems in humans and animals since the 1930s. "The real black, furry, nasty mess comes creeping back. It is terrible."

What you have just read, are quotes from the results of the hurricane Katrina that hit New Orleans. We are in deep concern for those in that area as well as in our low lands of North Carolina, that have had to put up with this, not only nuisance, but in some cases, causing deaths now and in the future.

This book is about the **"spiritual black mold."** To better understand this, I want to take you to seven things that God, notice, **"hates"** or **"dislikes or loathes,"** and the only corrective measure **is to have them blotted out by the blood of Jesus Christ.**

This is what this series of studies is about and how dangerous and eternally destructive these sins are to the Christian.

WE must be ever mindful that each of these deadly sins can destroy **not only the one involved** in them personally, but also the destruction of those that they are around and influence.

With these thoughts in mind, let's look at what the Bible teaches about these sins.

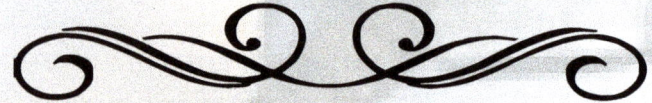

"We cleaned it up and he's been doing well about keeping things out of his closet, but the mold keeps creeping back in."

AUTHOR'S FORWARD

  If there was ever a time that this subject, "The Seven Deadly Sins of Proverbs," was needed; I am convinced it is today, and until our Lord Jesus Christ comes for His church.

  I make no claim for originality in these messages; neither do I make any apology for using all of the worthwhile material found in any other volumes or articles in doing research for the messages that I preached at our church, and that this book has its beginning.

Table of Contents

Dedication v
Introduction... vi
Author's Forward... ix

Chapter One
    The Seven Sins... 12

Chapter Two
    Sin #1 – Pride 29

Chapter Three
    Sin #2 – Lying 42

Chapter Four
    Sin #3 – Murder 55

Chapter Five
    Sin #4 – Mischievous Feet 74

Chapter Six
    Sin #5 – A Wicked Heart 98

Chapter Seven
    Sin #6 – Bearing False Witness........................... 108

Chapter Eight
    Sin #7 – The Danger of Sowing Discord! 128

Conclusion.. 150
Student Worksheets... 157

CHAPTER ONE

"THE SEVEN SINS"

Chapter One

There is a tendency in our world to avoid the negative. People just want to hear the good news; they are not interested in the bad. That is one way we can explain the success of people like these "feel good," everything is just "wonderful" and "you can do it."

They tell people how to live a better life now. They tell people how to find their purpose. But, they neglect to tell people about their sins. They prefer not to tell them about Hell. They omit telling them that God expects their lives to be one of holiness and godliness from His people, and that He will judge their wickedness and sin, in attitudes and actions. The bottom line in our churches today, is that people just do not want to hear that, yes, even Christians.

CREEPING BLACK MOLD

Let's look at these important verses because they **expose seven sinful attitudes and actions that God hates**. It seems to me that if God would declare His hatred for these sins, and He does in **Proverbs 6:16**, then we must be sure we hate these sins as well and be a trumpet sound to this world of Christianity. If there was ever a time that we must be sure that these sins are not a part of our lives it is in today's world.

Let me share with you the **thoughts** that present themselves to us in this text. These thoughts will teach us that what God hates should never be found in our lives. If we are His, we will hate what He hates, and we will love what He loves.

Before we look at each one of these "deadly sins," I want to describe briefly what they are, what is sin, what makes any of these seven deadly, what does God hate and what we can do.

What Does God Hate?

Well, we find that Solomon answers the question in our text that should be a guide for every believer in Christ to be aware of.

We in the church have failed to remind this generation that while God is love, He also has the capacity to hate. He hates sin, and He will judge it with the fierceness of His wrath. Today's generation is schooled in the teaching about an indulgent, soft-hearted God whose judgments are uncertain and who coddles those who break His commandments. This generation finds it difficult to believe that God hates sin.

Chapter One

I tell you that God hates sin just as a father hates a rattlesnake that threatens the safety and life of his child. God loathes evil and diabolic forces that would pull people down to a godless eternity just as a mother hates a venomous black widow spider that is found playing on the soft, warm flesh of her little baby.

It is His love for man, His compassion for the human race that prompts God to hate sin with such a vengeance.

He gave Heaven's finest that we might have the best; and He loathes with a holy abhorrence anything that would hinder our being reconciled to Him.

First: God Hates A Proud Look

The Bible says, *"Pride goeth before destruction, and a haughty spirit before a fall"* (Proverbs 16:18). It says, *"those who walk in pride He is able to put down"* (Daniel 4:37, NKJV). And again the Bible says, *"Behold, I am against you, O most haughty one!"* (Jeremiah 50:31, NKJV). We also find that it was this attitude that was maintained by the Pharisee in Luke 18:9-14.

The problem with a person who thinks he or she is perfect and they have no room for improvement will not come to or seek God.

It is said of Uzziah in II Chronicles 26:16 - *"But when he was strong, his heart was lifted up to his destruction: for he transgressed against the LORD his God, and went into the temple of the LORD to burn incense upon the altar of incense."*

CREEPING BLACK MOLD

During the Battle of the Wilderness in the Civil War, Union General John Sedgwick was inspecting his troops. At one point he came to an opening over which he gazed out in the direction of the enemy. His officers suggested that this was unwise and perhaps he ought to duck while passing the opening. "Nonsense," snapped the general. "They couldn't hit an elephant at this dist---------." A moment later Sedgwick fell to the ground, fatally wounded.

In almost every instance in the Bible, as well as in life, pride is associated with failure, not success. We hear a great deal about the inferiority complex, but the superiority complex of pride is seldom spoken of. Pride caused the fall of Lucifer, and he became Satan, the devil.

It is **PRIDE** that keeps thousands away from Christ today. What will my friends say? What will my family think? Will my reputation be affected if I become a Christian?

"And whoever exalts himself will be humbled, and he who humbles himself will be exalted."

Matthew 23:12

Jesus said, *"And whoever exalts himself will be humbled, and he who humbles himself will be exalted"* (Matthew 23:12, NKJV). The entrance to the Kingdom of Heaven is gained through your coming in humility.

The greatest act of humility in the history of the universe was when Jesus Christ stooped to die on the cross of Calvary. And before

Chapter One

anyone can get to Heaven, they must kneel at the foot of the cross and acknowledge that they are a sinner, that they have broken the commandments of God and that they need the grace of God in Christ. No one can come proudly to the Savior.

Will my reputation be affected if I become a Christian?

Second: God Hates A Lying Tongue

In the book **The Day America Told the Truth**, we read that 91 percent of those surveyed lie routinely about matters they consider trivial, and 36 percent lie about important matters; 86 percent lie regularly to parents, 75 percent to friends, 73 percent to siblings, and 69 percent to spouses.

Where did we learn to lie? Isn't it strange that children lie instinctively without being taught? The flagrant sins of fraud, embezzlement, slander, libel and breach of promise are the products of a lying heart.

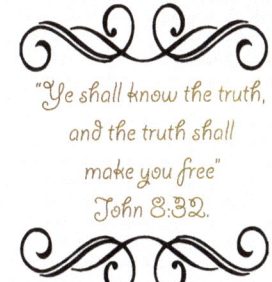
"Ye shall know the truth, and the truth shall make you free"
John 8:32.

Where did this blighting deceit come from? Jesus gave us the answer when He said to those who spoke a lie in His day, *"You are of your father the devil, and the desires of your father you want to do"* (John 8:44, NKJV). Human nature was warped and twisted in the fall

CREEPING BLACK MOLD

of Adam, but Jesus Christ, who is the truth, came saying, *"Ye shall know the truth, and the truth shall make you free"* (John 8:32).

In Revelation 21:8 we read, *"But the fearful, and unbelieving, and the abominable, and murderers, and whoremongers, and sorcerers, and idolaters, and all liars, shall have their part in the lake which burneth with fire and brimstone: which is the second death."*

I love this story: On a beautiful fall day, four students decided to go for a drive instead of showing up to class on time. When they did arrive, the students explained to the teacher that they had a flat tire. The teacher accepted the excuse, much to their relief. "Since you missed this morning's quiz, you must take it now," she said. "Please sit in the four corner seats in this room without talking." When they were seated, the teacher said, "On your papers write the answer to one question: 'Which tire was flat?'"

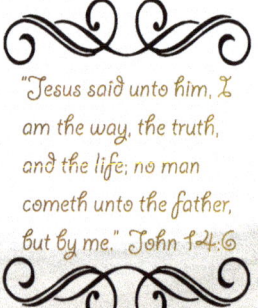

"Jesus said unto him, I am the way, the truth, and the life; no man cometh unto the father, but by me." John 14:6

Leviticus 19:11 - *"Ye shall not steal, neither deal falsely, neither lie one to another."*

Contrary to God's nature - I John 5:6 - *"This is he that came by water and blood, even Jesus Christ; not by water only, but by water and blood. And it is the Spirit that beareth witness,* **because the Spirit is truth**.*"*

Chapter One

John 14:6 - *"Jesus saith unto him, I am the way, the truth, and the life; no man cometh unto the Father, but by me."*
Where and when did we learn to lie?

Third: God Hates Hands That Shed Innocent Blood

The sixth commandment says, *"You shall not murder"* (Exodus 20:13, NKJV). Psychologists tell us that the seed of murder lurks in the heart of the most respected person.

The Bible says, *"Whoever hates his brother is a murderer, and you know that no murderer has eternal life abiding in him"* (I John 3:15, NKJV). Murder can be committed in many ways. You can murder your wife, your children and your friends by the poisonous venom of hatred, bitterness and envy through words and actions.

Not all murderers are behind bars. It so happens that only those who kill the body are punished by the law; but many who are free are just as guilty of destroying the lives, the personalities and the souls of others. The Bible says that you can strike someone with your tongue (Jeremiah 18:18) so then, according to this scripture you and I can ruin another person's reputation. God holds such people accountable for murder.

For just a moment now, let me briefly say, I will discuss this subject in more detail later that God hates abortion - -18 days after conception the heart beats on its own. At six weeks the fetus quick-

CREEPING BLACK MOLD

ly moves in the womb. Brain waves are present at eight weeks and the child grabs, swims freely, and the heartbeat is measurable. At 12 weeks cries, sucks thumb, sleeps and wakes, all organs and systems function, including mental. The unborn infant can definitely feel pain. From this point on nothing new develops; there is just growth and a maturing process.

> Exodus 20:13 - *"Thou shalt not kill."*
> Psalms 127:3 - *"Lo, children are an heritage of the LORD and the fruit of the womb is his reward."*

Here now is a sin that God hates that we sometimes overlook because we are "just flesh."

Fourth: God Hates Feet That Are Swift In Running To Mischief

There are evil thoughts in the hearts of all men but the devising and fabricating of them with a preoccupation that yields control to Satan is abhorrent to God.

Matthew 15:19 - *"For out of the heart proceed evil (grievous, hurtful deliberate) thoughts, murders, adulteries, fornications, thefts, false witness, blasphemies"* (NKJV).

"Lo, children are an heritage of the LORD and the fruit of the womb is his reward."
Psalms 127:3

Chapter One

This Scripture is teaching us that God hates a heart that devises evil imaginations. We must realize that thought is sown in the mind before it is reaped in the field of action. The law judges sin according to the act, but God judges us according to the evil of our hearts. *"Whoever looks at a woman to lust for her has already committed adultery with her in his heart," said Jesus* (Matthew 5:28, NKJV).

We are living in a day when men and women's imaginations are evil in the sight of God. The Bible says that He hates this. No person with an evil imagination can inherit the Kingdom of God. God hates evil imaginations. They lead to habits, habits lead to bondage, and bondage leads to death: *"The wages of sin is death"* (Romans 6:23).

We must be careful what we bury in our heart. To bury something does not mean it is dead. It may simply mean we have buried something alive that will devour and destroy us from within.

> II Corinthians 10:5 - *"Casting down imaginations, and every high thing that exalteth itself against the knowledge of God, and bringing into captivity every thought to the obedience of Christ."*

We must be careful what we bury in our heart.

Fifth: God Hates A Wicked Heart

It speaks of feet that quickly carry out what has already been devised in the heart.

CREEPING BLACK MOLD

This is more than falling or sliding into sin, which is common to all of us.

Evil thoughts and imagination, if nourished and fed, will eventually lead to sinful actions. There are people in every community who openly and flagrantly violate God's law. They boast that they are not hypocrites, and they make no pretense of being good. But this does not excuse them for their wickedness.

This is the execution of a premeditated act of sin. Read closely these verses; Proverbs 1:15-16 - *"My son, walk not thou in the way with them; refrain thy foot from their path: [16] For their feet run to evil, and make haste to shed blood."*

> Isaiah 59:7 - *"Their feet run to evil, and they make haste to shed innocent blood: their thoughts are thoughts of iniquity; wasting and destruction are in their paths"* (NKJV).

Six: God Hates False Witnesses

Literally this means – "he that breathes out or utters a false witness" or in the Southern vernacular, "outright lying!"

> Exodus 20:16 - *"Thou shalt not bear false witness against thy neighbor."* Perjury used in ruining the innocent.

> Matthew 26:59-61 - *"Now the chief priests, the elders, and all the council sought false testimony against Jesus to put him to death, but found none. Even though many false witnesses*

Chapter One

came forward, they found none. But at last came forward, they found none. But at last two false witnesses came forward and said, "This fellow said, 'I am able to destroy the temple of God and to build it in three days'" (NKJV).

Seven: God hates Sowers of Discord

James 3:2 - *"For in many things we offend all. If any man offend not in word, the same is a perfect man, and able also to bridle the whole body."*

The emphasis is on the man who intentionally seeks to destroy the harmony and unity among believers.

We seldom hear the slanderer, the libeler or the malicious gossip denounced. We have come to think that it is a harmless thing to sow discord in the office, the shop, the church or the home; but the Bible says that God hates discord and strongly denounces those who sow strife.

Ephesians 4:31 - *"Let all bitterness, and wrath, and anger, and clamor and evil speaking, be put away from you, with all malice."*

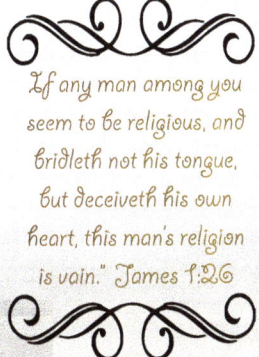

"If any man among you seem to be religious, and bridleth not his tongue, but deceiveth his own heart, this man's religion is vain." James 1:26

James 1:26 - *"If any man among you seem to be religious, and bridleth not his tongue, but deceiveth his own heart, this man's religion is vain."*

CREEPING BLACK MOLD

Now this brings us to a question that needs an answer.

What is sin? John tells us in his first epistle that *"all wrongdoing is sin...."* In other words, all **unrighteousness is considered sin and the Word of God is clear that which is not right, even to the point that James tells us,** *"to him that knoweth to do right and doeth not, to him it is sin."*

So, as you can see how horrible these sins are and how we must be careful that they do not invade our lives.....

What Can We Do?

"What can we do about these dreadful traits that are in our hearts?" you ask. There is little that you can do, but there is something God has done. The secret is found in the words of the Apostle Paul: *"Do not be conformed to this world, but be transformed by the renewing of your mind"* (Romans 12:2, NKJV). Jesus Christ, if received into your life, can make your tongue so that it will speak only that which is good. Only when Jesus Christ comes into your heart and transforms you, that there will be a change in your nature and then you'll love instead of hate. Gossiping, slandering and maligning will no longer provide pleasure. How can this be? I'll tell you. Christ, through His triumphant death on the cross, purchased for you a new lease on life. *"I have come that they might have life..."* (John 10:10, NKJV).

The Bible says, *"If we confess our sins, He is faithful and just to forgive us our sins, and to cleanse us from all unrighteousness"*

Chapter One

(I John 1:9). This is not just a theological theory; it actually works. It has worked in my own life. What is more, it will work for you. We have seen thousands of people whose lives have been transformed by the power of the Gospel of Jesus Christ, as we read in Romans 1:16. The same power of Christ can transform your life.

You say, "I'm guilty of all the things you have mentioned. Yes, the Bible says, *'all have sinned and fall short of the glory of God'*" (Romans 3:23, NKJV).

But no matter how guilty you may be and you may have broken every one of the commandments, God can and will forgive you today because Jesus Christ died on the cross for your sins. Yes, God hates the evil in your heart, but He loves you. Just as a parent despises the bad behavior of their child but still loves the child, God loathes the forces that would cause you to be lost, but He loves you with an infinite love.

However, this matter of salvation is not thrust upon you; it is a gift, and it must be duly and properly received. Here is the promise on which you may put your whole trust: *"But as many as received Him, to them He gave the right to become children of God, to those who believe in His name"* (John 1:12, NKJV).

At this moment you can receive Christ. He will forgive every sin that you have ever committed and give you new strength, new power over the temptations of life. But first you must renounce your sins, confess them and receive Christ into your heart. Will you do that right now? You can at this moment, and He will change your life.

CREEPING BLACK MOLD

"God hates the evil in your heart, but He loves you."

Chapter One

THOUGHTS:
_____
_____
_____
_____
_____
_____

ACTIONS:
_____
_____
_____
_____
_____
_____

"I have come that they might have life, and that they might have it more abundantly."
John 10:10

CREEPING BLACK MOLD

Right now ask yourself this question, "Have I asked Jesus to forgive me of all my sins and come into my life and save me?" If not, then why not right now before you go any further in this book, ask Christ to save you. Just pray this prayer from Romans 10:13, *"for whosoever shall call upon the name of the Lord shall be saved."*

Name: _____

If you are born again, and you harbor any of the sins we have discussed, why not now, bow and ask Christ to give you the complete victory in your life?

For the personal victory over these sins, sign below just as a reminder of your desire to be the witness Christ wants you to be.

Name: _____

CHAPTER TWO

SIN #1 - "PRIDE"

CREEPING BLACK MOLD

A great theologian once said, "A catalog of those things which are in a special manner odious to God, all which are generally to be found in because of Sin." We must remember that God hates sin; He hates every sin, He hates nothing but sin. But in this passage of Scripture we find certain sins which He does set apart that are provoking to Him. Matthew Henry says it this way, "those things which God hates are no thanks to us to hate in others, but we must hate them in ourselves."

In this chapter we will take a real close look at **sin number one**.

"Pride is the worst viper that is in the heart; it is the first sin that ever entered into the universe, and it lies lowest of all in the foundation of the whole building of sin, and is the most

Chapter Two

secret, deceitful and unsearchable in its ways of working, of any lusts whatsoever; it is ready to mix with everything; and nothing is so hateful to God, and contrary to the spirit of the Gospel, or of so dangerous consequence; and there is no one sin that does so much to let the devil into the hearts of the saints, and exposes them to his delusions" (Jonathan Edwards, Distinguishing Marks, Yale 4:277-78).

God hates pride (Proverbs 6:16-19; 16:5).

"These six things doth the Lord hate: yea, seven are an abomination unto him: A proud look (haughty eyes), a lying tongue, and hands that shed innocent blood, an heart that deviseth wicked imaginations, feet that be swift in running to mischief, A false witness that speaketh lies, and he that soweth discord among brethren." (Proverbs 6:16-19).

"Everyone that is proud (arrogant) in heart is an abomination to the Lord: though hand join in hand (be assured), he shall (will) not go unpunished" (Prov. 16:5). We read in James 4:16, *"But now ye rejoice (you boast) in your boastings (pride). All such rejoicing (boasting) is evil."*

What does it mean to say that God "hates" or that something is an "abomination" to Him?

1. When a human hates – we loathe things, seek to avoid them, destroy them, speak ill of them, vote against them, try to forget them, wish the worst for them.

CREEPING BLACK MOLD

2. When God hates – a pure, unalloyed, unmitigated, righteous displeasure, disgust, revulsion; to be an abomination to God, a stench, a repulsive and altogether putrid thing.

Pride is the precursor to virtually all other forms of sin; it is the soil in which all kinds of wickedness germinates and grows.

God is simply telling us that *"Pride goes before destruction and a haughty spirit before a fall. Better to be of a humble spirit with the lowly than to divide the spoil with the proud"* (Proverbs 16:18-19, NKJV).

Proverbs 18:12 (NKJV) - *"Before destruction the heart of a man (a man's heart) is haughty, before honor is humility (but humility comes before honor)."*

Proverbs 21:4 (NIV) - *"Haughty eyes and a proud heart, the lamp of the wicked, are sin."*

Proverbs 29:23 (NKJV) - *"A man's pride will bring him low, but the humble (he who is lowly) in spirit will retain (obtain) honor."* Is it really the case that pride is the precursor to or perhaps the root of most sin? Yes! Here are just a few.

Chapter Two

- **Envy** is a resentful awareness of an advantage enjoyed by another. But why does this evoke resentment in us? Why not joy? Because we don't want others to appear better than ourselves; or we think we are more worthy of that advantage or recognition than they are. Why? **Pride!**

- **Bitterness** is often the result of being personally offended or wronged by another. But why does that cause or bring bitterness? Because it either makes you look bad in the eyes of others or it deprives you of some blessing or comfort or convenience you think you deserve. **Pride!**

- **Strife** often flows out of a competitive desire to be number one, a desire to be acknowledged by others, a desire for power and authority. What is the source of such desire? **Pride!**

- **Deceit** is usually our strategy when we want to gain something for ourselves or when we want to hide something that might expose us. **Pride!**

- **Hypocrisy** is often the result of the fear of being seen and known for what we really are. Why do we experience such fear? **Pride!**

- **Slander** erupts when someone has been hurt or offended by another, or when you want to gain

CREEPING BLACK MOLD

acceptance and the only way is to lower others in the opinion of those whose favor you desire. Why? **Pride!**

➤ **Greed** comes from the desire to make more of one than God wishes or permits. Pride is the cold steel poker that stokes the fires of materialism. Someone once said that the reason why so many are going into debt is that their neighbors keep buying things they can't afford! But why do we desire to "keep up with the Jones'?" **Pride!** We can't stand the thought of people thinking we aren't as rich or successful or as talented and deserving as others.

Pride is that ugly part of our souls that causes us to be more concerned about ourselves and our reputation than we are about Christ and His.

Pride is that ugly part of our souls that causes us to be more concerned about ourselves and our reputation than we are about Christ and His.

Let's take a walk through the following scriptures as they reveal other observations about the truth about pride in Proverbs:

➤ It is destructive in its effects (Proverbs 30:11-14)
➤ It is an irritant to others (Proverbs 25:14)
➤ It often places a person beyond hope (Proverbs 26:12)

Let's take time to look at this sin:

Chapter Two

THE PROBLEM WITH PRIDE

Stop now and turn to Proverbs 16:18 and you will find out **WHAT PRIDE IS NOT**:

- Pride is not a good self-image.
- Humility is not thinking lowly of yourself; it is not thinking of yourself (Proverbs 29:23).
- Pride is not gratefulness for a job well done.

WHAT PRIDE IS:

- An attitude of independence from God.
- A spirit of ungratefulness to God.
- Esteeming ourselves better than others.

WHAT ARE THE INDICATORS OF A PROUD PERSON?

- A proud person becomes irritated when corrected for mistakes.
- A proud person accepts praise for things over which he or she has no control (i.e., beauty, talents, abilities).
- A proud person has an ungrateful spirit for all that God has done.
- A proud person often finds himself in competition with others.

Let me go a little further and expand the **SEVEN THINGS PRIDE WILL DO TO DEVASTATE AND RUIN YOUR CHRISTIAN TESTIMONY AND LIFE.**

CREEPING BLACK MOLD

First: Pride defies God, so let's spend some time in the following verses:

    Proverbs 6:16-19; Proverbs 16:5...with these verses read, this brings us to this question, why does God hate pride? We will do more investigation that God's words reveals on this subject.

Second: It was pride that made the devil the devil, Isaiah 14:13-16 and 1Timothy 3:6.

Third: It was pride that ruined the human race, Genesis 3:5, I Peter 5:5.

    As we study pride we see how pride defiles man, Proverbs 16:5 Proverbs 21:4 and Mark 7:21-22.

Fourth: Pride divides society, Proverbs 13:10, Proverbs 28:25.

Fifth: Pride dishonors life, Proverbs 11:2, Proverbs 15:33, Proverbs 18:12 and Proverbs 29:23.

Sixth: Pride destroys souls, Proverbs 15:25, Proverbs 16:18-19, Proverbs 18:12.

Seven: Pride is the road to ruin as we see in our present world today. As you look at these, why not do a Scripture search for each one:

    National ruin - _____
    Domestic ruin - _____

Chapter Two

Financial ruin - _____

Emotional ruin - _____

Spiritual ruin - _____

It was C. S. Lewis that said of pride, *"There is no fault which makes a man more unpopular, and no fault which we are more unconscious of in ourselves. And the more we have it in ourselves the more we dislike it in others."*

J. Vernon McGee said, *"Pride is the only disease known to man that makes everyone sick except the one who has it."*

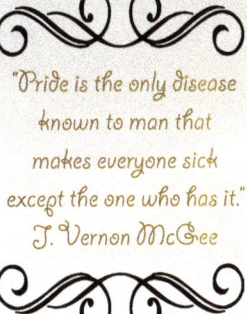
"Pride is the only disease known to man that makes everyone sick except the one who has it."
J. Vernon McGee

In this chapter I have tried to describe that pride is the worst malformation of all the monstrous things in creation. For instance:

> There is nothing lovely about it!

> It has no proportion, only everything in disorder and destruction!

> It is absolutely the reverse which God has made, which is pure and holy. It has been said the "pride, the first – born son of hell, is indeed like its parent, all unclean and vile, and in it there is neither form, fashion, nor comeliness."

CREEPING BLACK MOLD

Pride for the Christian should be unnatural to us, for what do we have to be proud of? What is it in us of whom we should glory?

Charles Spurgeon said, *"Nothing proves men so made as pride. For this they have given up rest, and ease and repose, to find rank and power among men: for this they have dared to rise their hope of salvation to leave the gentle yoke of Jesus and go toiling wearily along the way of life, seeking to save themselves by their own works and at last to stagger in the mire of fell despair."*

As we finish this chapter it is well to remember that God does not say that we are not to have honor. He has not forbidden it; He has only forbidden us to be proud of it.

Humility is to feel that we have no power of ourselves, but all we have and accomplish in this life comes from God. The answer is to die to self and to exalt, lift up high the Lord Jesus as all in all. It was the apostle John that said, "He must increase and I must decrease." Note the emphasis on the "**I**."

I ran across this while preparing this chapter and think it is a great truth about what pride can do if we are not careful.

Two ducks and a rather egotistical frog developed a friendship. When their pond dried up, the ducks knew they could easily fly to another location, but what of their friend the frog? Finally they decided to fly with a stick between their two bills, and with the frog hanging onto the stick by his mouth. All went well until a man looked up and saw them in the sky. *"What a clever idea,"* said the man. *"I wonder who thought of that?"*

Chapter Two

"I did," said the frog. Did you get the point?

Because Christians are followers of Christ, we should allow no room for pride:

- We take pride in our birth and position in life, but it's said of Jesus, He was a carpenter's son.
- We take pride in our possessions, but it's said of Jesus, "The Son of man hath no place to lay his head."
- We take pride in respectability, but it's said of Jesus, "Can anything good come out of Nazareth?"
- We take pride in our personal appearance, but it's said of Jesus, "He hath neither form nor comeliness."
- We take pride in our reputation, but it's said of Jesus, "Behold a man gluttonous and a winebibber."

"Pride goeth before destruction, and an haughty spirit before a fall. Better it is to be of a humble spirit with the lowly, than to divide the spoil with the proud."
Proverbs 16:18-19

CREEPING BLACK MOLD

- ➢ We take pride in our friendships, but it's said of Jesus, "He was a friend of publicans and sinners."
- ➢ We take pride in our independence, but Jesus gave Himself to people.
- ➢ We take pride in our position, but Jesus said, "I am among you as one who serves."
- ➢ We take pride in our degrees and learning, but Jesus never went to college and it's said of Him, "How knows this man letters having never learned to read?"
- ➢ We take pride in our success, but it's said of Jesus, "His own did not receive Him or believe on Him. He was despised and rejected."

Jesus Christ is the greatest example ever of humility. We who take the name of Christ need to live as Christ did—with humility, not pride.

As we finish this chapter it is well to remember that God does not say that we are not to have honor. He has not forbidden it; He has only forbidden us to be proud of it.

Chapter Two

THOUGHTS:

_____
_____
_____
_____
_____
_____
_____
_____
_____
_____

ACTIONS:

_____
_____
_____
_____
_____
_____
_____
_____
_____
_____
_____
_____

CREEPING BLACK MOLD

CHAPTER THREE

SIN #2 - "LYING"

Chapter Three

In this chapter we will take a close look at sin number two: ***"To tell the truth."***

    There was a television program back in the 1950's that I really enjoyed watching called "To Tell The Truth," hosted by a well known Hollywood personality, Bud Collyer, and the purpose of this program was to challenge a panel of four celebrities to correctly identify a described contestant who typically had an unusual occupation or experience. This "central character" was joined by two "imposters" who pretended to be that central character. The celebrity panelists questioned the team of challengers, with the imposters allowed to lie, but the central character "sworn to tell the truth." Host Bud Collyer: (at the end of every show with a giggle and a smile) "Don't you forget to tell the truth!?"

CREEPING BLACK MOLD

Well, this is exactly what God's Word is requiring each of us that know Christ as his or her personal Savior to do, "tell the truth." If we don't, look at the damage the cause of Christ will suffer.

I like what the late J. Vernon McGee said about this. He said, *"Have you ever noticed that there is far more said throughout the Bible about the abuse of the tongue than is said about the abuse of alcohol? The abuse of the tongue is something that is common to all races and all languages. People talk about a tongues movement. There is a big tongue movement today. Do you know what it is? 'A lying tongue, how tragic.'"*

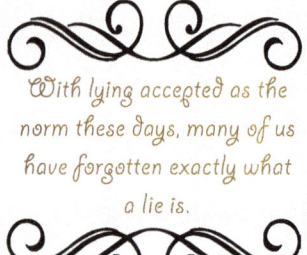

With lying accepted as the norm these days, many of us have forgotten exactly what a lie is.

That statement was said many years ago and still holds truth today in the year 2016. When one reads Isaiah chapter 59 and verses three and four, it sure seems to be describing America today.

Well, with lying accepted as the norm these days, many of us have forgotten exactly what a lie is; so let's pause to refresh our memories. Webster defines a lie as: "a false STATEMENT made with intent to deceive." And that's a pretty good start. But let's deepen our understanding by examining some of the many other shapes and forms that lies can take...

First, for instance, one form of lying could be called, *"the SILENT lie."* You see, you can lie or spread falsehood without even opening your mouth with the use of a lifted eyebrow, or a shrug of the

Chapter Three

shoulder intended to give a false impression. Proverbs 6:12-14 (NIV) describes this kind of lie when it says, *"A scoundrel and villain, who... winks with his eye, signals with his feet and motions with his fingers, who plots evil with deceit in his heart - he always stirs up dissension."* Friend you don't even have to do that; without moving a single muscle you can spread a lie and destroy anyone. Just by silently listening to people say things about another person that you know are not true and not speaking up and coming to their defense is to bear false witness.

Secondly, there also is lying by using **FLATTERY**. Proverbs 26:28 tells us that, **"A flattering mouth <u>worketh</u> ruin."** This simply means that giving **INSINCERE** praise saying something to someone's face that you would never say behind their back. It could be a complement to your pastor you might say, *"Wonderful message, pastor."* But, in the car on the way home you would say, *"That message had nothing and it was the most boring thing I have ever heard."* Kind of like the scene from an Andy Griffith show, where Andy said of his pastor, *"sometimes he is dry as dust."* Now, I am sure that no one reading this would ever do that to their pastor, but I'm just using it as an example! But we must be aware of when Psalm 55:21 talks about this kind of lie where it says, *"The words of his mouth were smoother than butter, but war was in his heart; His words were softer than oil, yet they were drawn swords"* (NKJV).

Then there is number **three**, **TRUTH** can be used to tell a lie. What? Can this be? Well, in John, chapter 8, Jesus is telling the Jewish religious leaders that He is the Son of God. And in response they were using truth to spread falsehood by saying,

CREEPING BLACK MOLD

"WE were not born of fornication," and they weren't, but by saying so they were inferring that Jesus WAS....that our Lord was the illegitimate son of Mary and not the Son of God. You see, we can even use TRUE statements to lie. A good illustration of this is when a captain on a ship disciplined a certain sailor on his crew for an infraction of the regulations. And from then on this sailor held a deep grudge against his captain. One day the captain was sick and this sailor was in temporary command. On this particular ship, it was the duty of the person in command to record the daily entry into the ship's log. This sailor entered the following statement, *"The captain was sober today."* Now that was the truth wasn't it, he was sober everyday...he didn't drink. However, writing that in the log was a selective truth. The sailor wrote this because he wanted to hurt the captain's reputation. His intent was to **deceive** people into believing that the captain had a drinking problem! Now, when we start getting this specific in our definition of what a lie is, many of us may wonder, *"What's the big deal about a little lying now and then? It has been said of a latest pole, that ninety-one percent of Americans lie regularly; and that sixty-three percent of men and fifty-two percent of women have lied to protect themselves and worse is that over forty percent have lied on job applications and friend, Christians are not immune from the temptation. As a Christian we must follow what Ephesians 4:25 says and it tells us to 'put away lying.'"*

Let's stop here for a moment to ask and answer four questions.

WHAT IS LYING?

Chapter Three

The root idea of lying is *"falsehood and deception."* One has said, *"To deceive, or attempt to deceive, by a lie."* Again, *"A lie is a false statement deliberately presented as being true; something meant to deceive or give one a wrong impression."*

In a broader sense, whatever is not what it professes to be is a lie. False impressions are created to deceive and sometimes harder for one to detect, for instance:

- Self-righteousness - Matthew 23:27-28
- Religious lies - II Corinthians 11:13-15
- Hypocrisy - I Timothy 4:1-2
- Doctrines of men - Romans 1:25

Then there is the sin of the subtle lie, again examples:

- *"I am very religious"* - James 1:26
- *"I do not sin"* - I John 1:8
- *"I know Him"* - I John 2:3-4

"A lie is a false statement deliberately presented as being true; something meant to deceive or give one a wrong impression."

That is why there needs to be on a daily basis a careful self-examination of one's self (II Corinthians 13:5).

That brings us to our next question.

WHY DO PEOPLE LIE?

CREEPING BLACK MOLD

First, according to the gospel of Matthew, chapter 26 and verses 69-74, it is out of **FEAR**! Fear of what men may do to us and the suffering that truth may bring. Yet, we are told in Luke, chapter 12 and verses 4-5 that we are to **"fear God and not man"** so we are not to lie out of fear. **Truth never needs defense.**

"Fear God and no man."
"Truth never needs defense."

Secondly, there is also another reason that man lies and that is to shirk their responsibility as we find in Luke 14:18. Whenever we begin to make excuses for our disobedience, we definitely display displeasure of God's will in our lives. So then we lie, we lie to ourselves, to others and most of all to God.

Thirdly, man lies to hurt someone. In Colossians 3:8-9 we find that malicious lies are intended to destroy, damage or to discredit someone. Two of the greatest examples of this is found in the book of Genesis, chapter 39 and verses 13-20 where Potiphar's wife accused Joseph and in Matthew, chapter 26 and verses 59-61 when the chief priest and elders lied to cause the reason for death to Jesus.

Fourthly, man lies to gain an advantage or to get gain. If we are not careful we get caught up in the desire to get financial gain at whatever the cost. Too many Christians are engrossed with money that they begin to leave God out of their lives when Sunday is the day to serve God. As a boy back in the 1950's, I know, in the old days, on Sunday in my hometown no public business was open during the

Chapter Three

church services. Then after the noon hour only a local pharmacy, and gas station would be open until four pm and then close; by the way, no restaurants were open at all. Why? Sunday was respected as "The Lord's Day." Now I know that in this day we live in, due to the increase of business, many have to work on Sundays, i.e., hospitals, emergency such as rescue, fire and law enforcements, but not all does. We have a young man in our church that works for the highway patrol and when he is on duty, and in our area, he takes his lunch hour to be in church. Here is a young man with his priorities right and his love for his Savior and his church. My point here is, too many Christians will desire to work on Sundays for more financial gain, when they could be in church.

Fifthly, too many Christians lie for *"what is good for me."* In other words, *"the end justifies the means"* yet, we find in the book of Romans, chapter 3 and verse 8 where it reads, *"let us do evil that good may come to us."* If we look closely in the word of God, we are told that God defines and tells us what is good and what we are to do. There is no good reason, God given reason, for lying!

A good study of the Bible on this subject, we find that God warns us not to lie and to turn away from the evil of such, and He tells us that lying is disgusting to Him and that He will punish all liars.

Let each of us take heed to Ephesians, chapter 4 and verse 25 that says, ***"put away lying."***

With these said: What are consequences of our not telling the truth?

CREEPING BLACK MOLD

1. **Well, first off...when we lie WE HURT OURSELVES.**

   I Peter 3:10 (NIV) says, *"Whoever would love life and see good days must keep his tongue from evil and his lips from deceitful speech."* When we lie we don't **ENJOY** the life God has given us. We don't **SEE** good days. We become suspicious of other people, wondering if they are truthful with us. Then we live our days in constant fear that we will be found out and we are usually forced to tell more and more lies to cover our deceitful tracks. Martin Luther said, *"A lie is like a snowball. The longer it is rolled on the ground, the larger it becomes."* And no matter how good we are at "sin," lies always catch up with us eventually. God warned us of this in Numbers 32:23 when He said, *"You can be sure that your sins will find you out."* Lying destroys character and can become a habit. The more you lie the more **EASILY** you lie. We forget what the truth is and lose ourselves in a web of deceit. We become less real...less genuine. *"A farmer once cut down a huge tree that was on his land. It looked good from the outside but he discovered that the heart of the tree was rotten. He looked closely at it and found a huge old nail. Apparently years ago someone had driven it in the tree and it had caused the heart of the tree to rot."*

   "When we lie, we hurt ourselves...."

   This is how it is with the life of the person who lies. His life becomes a hollow shell and his spiritual life withers and dies. So when we lie, we hurt ourselves...

2. **But we also hurt our RELATIONSHIPS WITH OTHERS.**

   A wife once asked her husband, *"Why don't you play golf with Jim anymore."* Her husband replied, *"Would you play golf with a man*

Chapter Three

who moved the golf ball with his foot when you weren't watching?" His wife said, *"Well, no. I wouldn't."* Her husband said, *"Well, neither will Jim."* We are social beings. We need relationships to be happy. We want to get along with one another and live in harmony but this is not possible if we cannot trust one another. When the truth is not a "given" factor in any relationship, disappointment, heartache, and insecurity are the inevitable result. Lying knocks the foundation out from under any relationship whether it is with a spouse or a child or a best friend. And, among the most significant relationships that are damaged by our lies...are our relationships with other Christians in our church family and it not only drives them from our fellowship but many times they never go back to a local church for not wanting to be hurt again. Writing to the church at Ephesus Paul said, *"Wherefore putting away lying, speak every man truth with his neighbour: for we are members one of another"* (Ephesians 4:25).

3. **The WORST damage caused by lying is that it PUSHES US AWAY FROM GOD.**

We find in Proverbs (NIV), chapter 12 and verse 22 where it says, *"the Lord detests lying lips, but He delights in men who are truthful."* So we know how God feels about lying, don't we? Today, we hear the saying, *"God is love,"* but some make the mistake of thinking that God is only love. Love is but one of God's many character traits. He is also **TRUTH**. In John, chapter 17 verse 3, we read, *"the only TRUE God."* Jesus said, *"I am the way and the truth"* in John, chapter 14 and verse 6. The Holy Spirit defines what it means to be good, holy and pure; He also defines what it means to be true. So from God's word, God cannot tolerate falsehood. In some way it's like a person who has allergies. Our grandson, Seth, is allergic to

CREEPING BLACK MOLD

dust from fresh evergreen trees. His immune system is overly sensitive to this stuff. It attacks in the same way that it would an invading bacteria or virus. His eyes water and itch. Seth and dust and evergreen trees don't mix. This is the same way it is with God and **ANY SIN** in the life of the Christian.

God doesn't just choose to dislike sin. By His very nature, he will not tolerate the presence of sin. So when we callously, thoughtlessly lie in the course of everyday life, we are separating ourselves from Him and we move farther away and we become like those people Paul was describing in Romans, chapter 1, when he said, *"they exchange the truth of God for a lie."*

There is a need for daily examination for each of us to be honest in all that we do.

Now I could not leave this chapter without giving the solution to how to overcome lying.

"Whatsoever things are true, honest, just, pure, lovely, of good report, think on these things."

First: Love the truth. In the 21st Century this is almost something that is foreign to our lifestyle and to have this there must, first of all, be a heart change and love for the truth.

Second: Learn the truth. Read Philippians 4 and verse 8 below. Saturate your mind with good things like the Word of God for the truth will set you free.

Chapter Three

"Finally, brethern, whatsoever things are **true**, whatsoever things are **honest**, whatsoever things are **just**, whatsoever things are **pure**, whatsoever things are **lovely**, whatsoever things are of **good report**; if there be any virtue, and if there be any praise, **think on these things**."

Thirdly: Live the truth. Meditate on Ephesians, chapter 4 and verse 25. What does it say to you?

_____

_____

_____

_____

_____

Think about this, what if your eyes lied to your legs about where you could walk? What if your ears lied to your brain about when it sounded safe to walk across a busy street? If your body worked in this deceitful way it wouldn't be long before it was no longer functioning. And the same is true of the church. When we don't put away **"truthLESSness,"** people become afraid to reach out. They become hesitant to move because they don't know whom to trust. We have to be able to trust one another here of all places...if we are to move forward as the Body of Christ....functioning as His hands and feet in your community and world.

CREEPING BLACK MOLD

THOUGHTS:
_____
_____
_____
_____
_____
_____
_____
_____

ACTIONS:
_____
_____
_____
_____
_____
_____
_____
_____
_____
_____

"Lying pushes us away from God!"

CHAPTER FOUR

SIN #3 - "MURDER"

CREEPING BLACK MOLD

We now turn in our study of seven of the deadliest sins **and it is the sin of murder - the act of ending an innocent human life**. We'll be using three very familiar texts as a basis of our study. Exodus 20:13, Proverbs 6:16-17 and Matthew 5:21-22. There are six things the LORD hates, seven that are detestable to Him: haughty eyes, a lying tongue, hands that shed innocent blood.

> *Matthew 5:21, 22 (NIV) – "You have heard that it was said to the people long ago, 'Do not murder, and anyone who murders will be subject to judgment.' But I tell you that anyone who is angry with his brother will be subject to judgment. Again, anyone who says to his brother, 'Raca,' is answerable to the Sanhedrin. But anyone who says, 'You fool!' will be in danger of the fire of hell."*

Chapter Four

As you can see, the Bible plainly says that this sin that is **LITERALLY** deadly; God's Word says that **MURDER** is wrong. It is clearly against His will. But before we go any further in our study of this particular deadly sin, first let's be sure we understand what the Bible does **NOT** say.

1. **One thing it does not say is this, it does not say, "You shall not KILL."**

    I mean an accurate translation of Exodus 20:13 (NIV) would be, *"You shall not MURDER."* The Hebrew word here is *"ratsach"* and it is a word that refers to unauthorized, premeditated and violent killing or murder. I point this out because there is of course a vast difference between murder and killing. If this commandment were to be taken as a blanket prohibition of ALL killing, then it would be wrong to kill dangerous animals, poisonous snakes, or even pesky insects.

    You may remember that one of the great missionaries to Africa was Dr. Albert Schweitzer who spent his life there spreading the gospel. He also built a mission hospital in Lambarene, Africa. Well, Schweitzer took this command to mean that killing anything was forbidden so he strictly forbade the killing of even so much as a fly or a mosquito. Yet, ironically the good doctor and his associates were in Africa in part to save lives by destroying the lives of disease-bearing organisms and microbiological life forms. Well, Schweitzer was

CREEPING BLACK MOLD

mistaken in his understanding of this Biblical prohibition because...

2. **Another thing the Bible does not forbid is the taking of ANIMAL life.**

Now, God's Word **DOES** teach the humane treatment of animals. Proverbs 12:10 (NIV) says, *"A righteous man cares for the needs of his animal..."* But the Bible gives us the right to kill animals for food. In Genesis 9:3 (NIV) God says, *"Everything that lives and moves will be food for you. Just as I gave you the green plants, I now give you everything."* Scripture records that Jesus ate fish on numerous occasions and as a good Jewish man He would also have eaten meat at Passover. So the Bible does not forbid the killing of animals for food.

3. **Neither does the Bible prohibit WAR.**

"The only thing for evil to triumph, is for good men to do nothing."

You see, whereas war is always wrong, sadly enough in a sinful culture and world of greed and power, war is often necessary to insure that people will be treated justly by others. For over fifty years of preaching, I have mentioned that in this fallen world of ours, **FREEDOM** is something we will always have to **FIGHT** to **EARN**

Chapter Four

and **DEFEND** to **KEEP**. It was Aarron Burr that said, *"The only thing for evil to triumph, is for good men do nothing."* We must defend our freedom even if it means war and our great nation has done this for hundreds of years; yes, even at the loss of lives that you and I have the freedom to worship God. You may not realize this, but since the days of Saint Augustine and Thomas Aquinas, the church has worked to develop the concept of a *"just war."* But basically a *"just war"* is a war that is waged only as a last resort when all other efforts at diplomacy have failed. It is a war that defends that which is right or punishes that which is wrong. For a war to meet the *"just war"* criteria it must have a *"just cause,"* such as ending Hitler's aggression or freeing people from the tyranny of cruel dictators like Saddam Hussein, and even the late Ben Laden. I mean, the goal of a *"**JUST** war"* is to make things better for the nations involved. For this reason a nuclear war would fail to meet the standards of the *"just war"* theory.

In any case, the Bible's commands not to murder are not to be interpreted as a stand against war. Sometimes war, as bad as it is, is necessary for the greater good. This is one reason Jesus said, *"...there will be wars and rumors of war..."* (Matthew 24:6, NIV).

4. **We should also note that the Bible does not prohibit the DEATH penalty.**

CREEPING BLACK MOLD

In fact, capital punishment for the murder of an innocent person is mandated in Scripture. By the way, this is the only mandate that is repeated in each of the first five books of the Bible (Genesis 9:6, Exodus 21:12, Leviticus 24:17, Numbers 35:31, Deuteronomy 19:21). It is first mentioned when Noah exited the ark and God said, *"Whoever sheds the blood of a man, by man shall his blood be shed"* (Genesis 9:6, NIV).

However, we should also note that the Bible contains very careful guidelines to protect people who were wrongfully accused of murder. In Bible times, cities of refuge were designated as safe places to which an individual could flee if he had accidentally ended the life of another. He would find protection there and be given a chance to explain what happened.

Deuteronomy 19:15 also says that at least two witnesses must see the crime before a person can be charged with murder. And circumstantial evidence was not valid in a Jewish court. So, as it says in Exodus 23:7 (AV) steps were always taken **NOT** to *"...condemn to death (execute) the innocent and the righteous..."* But, in any case, the Bible does not prohibit capital punishment. We need to realize that there is a great difference between the murder of an innocent person and society's determination to end the life of the individual who has intentionally killed another human being.

Humanity must realize that a capital punishment law underscores how precious human life is because; it serves as a deterrent to protect life. The philosophy behind capital

Chapter Four

punishment says that if an individual shows that he does not cherish human life he must forfeit his own, so that others will not lose their right to life at his hands.

OKAY - now that we've clarified things when it comes to what the Bible does **NOT** forbid, let's look at what it does; God's Word does indeed forbid **MURDER**.

Do you remember our text from Proverbs? It says, God hates, *"Hands that shed innocent blood."*

"God hates - Hands that shed innocent blood."

Well let's try to understand why God feels this way. Why would He include in the Ten Commandments and other Scriptures this prohibition against murder?

1. **First, we need to understand that in the Bible, DEATH is described as God's ENEMY.**

    First Corinthians 15:26 (NIV) says, *"The last **ENEMY** to be destroyed is **DEATH**."* Now, think about that. Why would death be referred to as the enemy of God? Well, here's why, death is the enemy of God because death destroys life, in contrast to God, the Creator and Author of life. The Bible tells us that sin nor pain, disease, nor **DEATH** was part of God's original plan for man. I mean, death was not God's idea. No, death entered the world because of sin, and since then death has been Satan's cause, not God's. Remember? In John 8:44,

CREEPING BLACK MOLD

Satan, the adversary of God, is described as a murderer - a killer - a being who is opposed to God's purposes.

I for one believe Jesus was referring to Satan in John 10:10 (NIV) when He said, *"The thief comes only to steal and kill and **DESTROY;** I have come that they may have **LIFE**, and have it to the full."*

So God values **LIFE** - not death. Scripture clearly teaches that God is pro-life. Death is the enemy from His perspective. So you see, when we murder, whether it be with a handgun or with a doctor's hands in an abortion clinic or in a hospice center by actively euthanizing a brain-damaged girl, we are opposing God Himself.

2. **God has given us this law to remind us that human life is not ours to take.**

Everything we have and are - including our lives - belong to **GOD**, not us, so when we end a life prematurely, whether it be ours or another's, we have overstepped our bounds. Job 14:5 (NIV) says, *"Man's days are determined; you (Oh Lord) have decreed the number of his months and have set limits he cannot exceed."* This and other texts tell us that God - the Author of life - determines the length of our lives, not the other way around. I mean, we are not the Lord of human life - God is! Our lives are a gift from God that we are to carefully steward from the womb to the tomb - not end when they become inconvenient.

Chapter Four

There are many instances in Scripture where an individual wanted to end his life at a time of his own choosing and in each of these instances God said, *"NO, that's not for you to decide."* For example, **MOSES** - that Prince of Egypt - grieved about the burden the Lord had given him. He looked at his people grumbling about their food and their living conditions, complaining so much that old Moses finally reached his limit. He'd had it and, in Numbers 11:15, he said to God, *"If this is how You are going to treat me, put me to death right now. (I want to die)!"* But that wasn't Moses' call to make. The Lord was not finished with Moses yet! He went on to lead his people through the wilderness and to the boundaries of the Promised Land.

Then there was that amazing day when **ELIJAH** killed the prophets of Baal, yet when the evil Queen Jezebel swore she was going to get even, the fearless Elijah ran into the wilderness, sat down under a juniper tree, and cried out, *"I have had enough, Lord, take my life; I am no better than my ancestors"* (1 Kings 19:4, NIV). But that wasn't for Elijah to decide. His life wasn't his to take. So the Lord sent an angel to supply him with food and water - essential ingredients to life. The Lord was not finished with Elijah yet.

Consider **JOB**. He had boils all over his body. His flesh was eaten by worms. His skin was oozing and decaying like rotten turnips. He was so shriveled and thin that his bones were sticking out...and he had gnawing pains and frightening dreams. Under such circumstances, most of us would cry out,

CREEPING BLACK MOLD

as Job did, *"Oh that God would be willing to crush me, to let loose His hand and cut me off"* (Job 6:9, NIV)! But the Lord was not finished with Job yet, either. I wonder if we had been with Job in his pain - wracked, miserable situation, would we have taken away his food and water, and allowed him to starve, dehydrate, and die. Well, to do so would be opposed to God's purposes for He restored Job's health and gave him many more years of productive life - and God determines productive life - not us! The plain fact is, our lives aren't ours to take - they are God's. He determines when they begin and when they end - not us. Our moments and days and years - are His - not ours.

"Our lives do not belong to us."

How would you feel if your neighbor decided your house was an inconvenience to him? It blocked his access to park land. So, one day while you were gone to work he hired those Extreme Home Makeover Edition guys to bring their heavy equipment in to level your house and haul all the debris away. How would you feel if you got home and found a vacant lot where your home once stood? I'm sure you'd be so angry and you'd find multiple ways to tell your neighbor he had overstepped his bounds. That wasn't his call to make! That was your house! Well, that's what God is saying here. Our lives do not belong to us. We don't say when to end them. As Creator and absolute Owner, that is His call.

3. **Another reason God wants us to see MURDER as**

Chapter Four

a sin is because each human life is UNIQUE - and we see this from the very beginning in the WAY humans were created.

Look at the first chapter of Genesis and you will see that humans were created in a way that differed from the way all other things were created. In each **OTHER** creative act God said, *"Let there be,"* and it was so. God spoke and creation occurred but the creation of human life begins differently. God says, *"Let us MAKE man..."* So God didn't just speak us into existence as He did everything else. No, He **MADE** us! To create the first human, verse 7 of Genesis 2 (NIV) says, *"God formed the man from the dust of the ground and breathed into his nostrils the breath of life, and the man became a living being."* God did not *"BREATHE the breath of life"* into any other creature, so human life **IS** unique, in that it was made differently. Only we have living **SOULS**. We are not just a body!

Another thing, Genesis also records the fact that after God made something, like the sun or the oceans, the Scripture said, *"And God saw that it was good."* But when He created **HUMAN LIFE** He said that it was not just "good" but *"VERY good."* So, in God's eyes human life IS unique in that it is more highly esteemed than any other form of life. The Genesis account also says that human life was created on the last day of God's creative work. In other words, it was the climax - the paramount - of all the rest of creation, as if everything else He created was made with us in mind.

CREEPING BLACK MOLD

Ecclesiastes 3:11 (NIV) says that God *"....has set (planted) eternity in the hearts of men..."* This means that, unlike other created beings, we can affect much more than just our short lives. We can actually *"lay up for ourselves treasures in heaven."* Each human life is unique in that it can do things that have eternal significance.

Here's another thing to note - the Bible says that **ONLY** man was made in God's image. Now, since God is spirit, this doesn't mean we are physically like God. So, the fact that we are made in the image of God means we have similar inner qualities, the ability to reason, to enter into relationships...especially to relate to God. No other created thing has the ability to relate to our Creator as we do - not even angels.

By the way, do you realize that human beings are the closest thing in all creation to God? Psalm 8:5 says that man is *"a little lower than heavenly beings."* Some translations say *"a little lower than angels"* but the word translated *"angels"* or *"heavenly beings"* is "**ELOHIM**"...one of the words for God. So this verse actually says that we are created *"a little lower than* **ELOHIM** *- God Himself."* I mean, the ranking order in creation is not **GOD**, angels, humans. It is God, humans, angels. In God's sight angels aren't of greater value than human beings; in fact the reverse is true. Angels are never said to be created in God's image. Only man is given this distinction.

The fact is, it is wrong to murder a human being because each human life is unique. Think of it this way, each

Chapter Four

human being is an original, one of a kind masterpiece - irreplaceable. That includes you! You are priceless in value! You are special!! Did you know researchers have discovered that there are at least 18,000 different personality traits? The possible combinations of these various traits are limitless. So, hear this, you **ARE** unique! There is not another person in this world like you. There has never been and never will be. God did not create carbon copies. He only makes originals.

The next time you are in church or some outdoor activity, look at the person sitting next to you, in front and behind you, that individual is an original. Look all around you, there's another priceless masterpiece. I mean, each Sunday when we gather we turn that room into God's art gallery of irreplaceable one-of-a-kind masterpieces. So you see, it would be a crime to end any life. Each human being is priceless because each human being is unique - with unique insights and wisdom and talents.

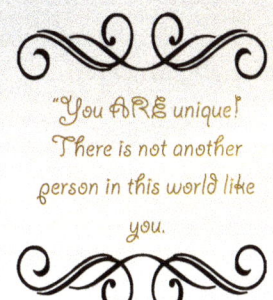

"You ARE unique! There is not another person in this world like you."

This reminds me of a story I came across while preparing this series for my church that told of a conversation between two doctors. One doctor said to another, *"About the termination of a certain pregnancy, I want your opinion. The father was syphilitic. The mother was tuberculosis. Of the four children born, the first was blind, the second died, the*

CREEPING BLACK MOLD

third was deaf and dumb, and the fourth was also tuberculosis. What would you have done about this last pregnancy?" "I would have ended it." said the second. **"Then you would have murdered Beethoven."** said the first.

This illustrates the fact that each human life is precious - murder is a foolish waste.

4. **But you know, the greatest proof of the extreme - value of each and every human life is seen in the fact that God has said that each life is equal in value to that of His only SON.**

You know, we judge the seriousness of the crime of theft by the value of the items stolen. Inexpensive theft would be a misdemeanor, but taking more valuable property would be a felony. We must realize that the more valuable the theft the greater the crime and the greater the punishment. Well, as I said, human life is unique and that makes it valuable; but, the thing that really shows its value is this fact that in God's eyes each life is worth the life of His own **SON**. This is an estimation of human worth beyond our comprehension. I mean, God treasures you and me more than any other thing He created and this is indicated by the fact that He not only loved us enough to create us, He also loved us enough to pay the unbelievable cost of redeeming us! Romans 5:8 (NIV) says, *"God demonstrates His own love for us in this (He shows how much He valued human life in this): while we were still sinners, Christ died for us."* So, as C. S. Lewis once wrote, there is no such

Chapter Four

thing as a *"mere mortal."* The words to that song we sang as children are so true, *"Red, yellow, black and white, they **ARE** precious in His sight."*

Now maybe you read all this and think, I agree with you, murder is wrong but I never murdered anyone and am not planning on it, so I'm in the clear here.

Well, the fact is you're not in the clear - neither am I. We're all guilty of committing this particular deadly sin. I say this because in the text we read earlier from the Sermon on the Mount, Jesus said even our anger directed at other people can make us guilty of cheapening a priceless human life. You see, our Savior taught that murder is more than an act. It is an attitude. Jesus says that *"anyone who is angry with his brother will be subject to judgment. And anyone who says to his brother, 'Raca,' is answerable to the Sanhedrin or anyone who says, 'You fool!' will be in danger of the fire of hell."*

Now, let's go back to the word *"Raca."* It was really more of a **SOUND** than a **WORD**. It was a clearing of the throat as though to say, "I spit on you." And to call another person a *"worthless fool"* was the same as writing them off all together. Jesus said this was as bad as actually killing a person because when we get this angry with someone, then deep down inside we are thinking that this person doesn't deserve to be alive. In this instant of anger we are saying, *"I don't want to have anything to do with this person. As far as I'm concerned my life would be better if his life would end."*

CREEPING BLACK MOLD

You know, we are a lot like the Pharisees of Jesus' day in that we would rather deal with **EXTERNALS**, but Jesus is not satisfied with that. He wants to deal with **INTERNAL** things. He wants to talk about what is happening in our hearts. He knows that long before you or I would murder someone, we would begin the process with our thoughts. Ron Mehl writes, *"Jesus deals with the **ROOT** of this commandment, not just its fruit. He's not content to trim off the nettles and poison oak in our lives close to the ground. No, He wants to uproot the whole poisonous weed."*

Jesus taught that the root of murder is anger - hateful, people - dishonoring anger. Well, let me ask you, have you ever been so angry with another person that you wished they were dead? As you listened to Michael Schiavo's attorney defend the act of starving Terri, did you ever get so angry you wished he would starve himself? Did you think, *"If he likes ending life so much I wish he'd end his own?"* Have you ever gotten so angry at a sibling that you wished you were an only child? Have you ever been so mad you lost it and wished your boss or a co-worker had never been born? Ever wished someone driving too slow as you hurried to work wasn't there?

I think if we were honest, we'd all have to admit this sin and ask for God's forgiveness because there are times when each of us devalues human life, if not with our actions, then with our thoughts. One more quick thought-the best way to honor God's law against murder is to do the opposite - to cherish each life - to love people, even those who are hard to love.

Chapter Four

Finally, let me address anyone who may already have had an abortion or may have urged someone else to have an abortion. Perhaps you did it in ignorance or bad decision making, but now you realize that you committed a serious sin in God's sight, well the good news is that Jesus Christ came into the world to save sinners.

Can Jesus help you? Yes, He can. *"For whosoever shall call upon the name of the Lord shall be saved"* (Romans 10:13).

Before the printing of this book, we had a special service at our church supporting the *"Sanctity of Life."* In this service was a young lady that in July of 2011 chose not to abort her little girl. I have a picture where she was kissing her little daughter on the top of her little head. It is on one of my book shelves in my church office and every time I leave my office, I never ceased to pray for her. In April of 2013, the mother was here on that special day with her little girl and now expecting her second child; and she is happily married and as she exited our platform she said, *"I am so glad I did not abort my baby."* Yes, God does forgive and forget. Never forget this, what a wonderful, forgiving God we have.

Why not spread this message of LOVE?

CREEPING BLACK MOLD

But you know, the greatest proof of the extreme-value of each and every human life is seen in the fact that God has said that each life is equal in value to that of **HIS ONLY SON.**

"For whosoever shall call upon the name of the Lord shall be saved."
Romans 10:13

Chapter Four

THOUGHTS:

_____
_____
_____
_____
_____
_____
_____
_____
_____
_____

ACTIONS:

_____
_____
_____
_____
_____
_____
_____
_____
_____
_____

CHAPTER FIVE

SIN #4 – "MISCHIEVOUS FEET"

Chapter Five

Feet are Swift In Running To Mischief – Someone said *"The heart blazes the trail the feet follow."* When *"wicked imaginations"* are formed in the heart, the feet will be quick to carry them out, Isaiah 59:7.

The paths the feet follow in life reveal the condition of the heart, Matthew 12:33. When your feet carry you to do evil; when they carry you to worldly places; when they carry you around the country spreading lies, rumors and gossip; when they carry you from bed to bed, from pleasure to pleasure, your feet reveal the condition of your heart. What you do is what you are!

"Feet that be swift in running to Mischief." Proverbs 6:18b

CREEPING BLACK MOLD

It speaks of feet that is quick to carry out what has already been devised in the heart.

This is more than falling or sliding into sin, which is common to all of us. This is the execution of a premeditated act of sin.

> *Proverbs 1:15-16 - "My son, walk not thou in the way with them; refrain thy foot from their path: for their feet run to evil, and make haste to shed blood."*
>
> *Isaiah 59:7 - "Their feet run to evil, and they make haste to shed innocent blood: their thoughts are thoughts of iniquity; wasting and destruction are in their paths."*

"Feet that run rapidly to evil" are also hated by God. Catch the note of urgency and energy involved in their crime. They eagerly seize each opportunity because they want to hatch and fulfill their schemes quickly. The proportion of power that evil has over a man is seen in his eagerness to do it.

As we look at the lesson in this chapter, I want to share with you what the Word of God has to say about <u>*"What Kind of Feet God's People Ought to Have.*</u>*"*

I. **God's People Should Have <u>Cleansed</u> Feet (John 13:1-17).**

Chapter Five

One of the most intriguing characters in the New Testament is a man by the name of Epaphroditus. His story can be found in Philippians 2:25-30. Epaphroditus is interesting because he was a rare individual. Epaphroditus is interesting because he was a servant. That text tells us that Epaphroditus served the Apostle Paul, verse 25. He was very sick, but still he was worried about the Philippians because he knew they were worried about him, verse 26.

Paul goes on to tell us that the sickness Epaphroditus suffered came about because he was a servant. In verse 30 Paul says, *"Because for the work of Christ he was nigh unto death, not regarding his life, to supply your lack of service toward me."* The phrase *"not regarding his life"* is interesting. It is a gambling term. It means *"to recklessly expose one's life to danger."* In gambling terminology, it means *"to risk everything on one roll of the dice."*

Epaphroditus willingly placed his life on the line to serve Paul. He gambled everything for Jesus Christ so that the man of God would be served and the Philippian church, which had sent him to Paul in the first place, would be well represented.

"What Kind of Feet God's People Ought to Have."

Around 250 AD, a group of early Christians around ancient Carthage called themselves **"The Gamblers."** They

CREEPING BLACK MOLD

named themselves after Epaphroditus. These people went into the city of Carthage, during the height of the plagues, when bodies were stacked head high along the streets, and carried the dead outside the city and buried them. They risked their very lives to serve the citizens of Carthage, many of whom hated them because they were Christians. These people possessed the same spirit that dwelt in Epaphroditus.

Where did Christians like Epaphroditus and **"The Gamblers"** get their desire to serve others? After all, it is not a natural desire. I believe they got their spirit of selfless service from the Lord Jesus Christ.

"No artist's skill can ever bring out on a canvas that distance from the throne of God..."

There is no artist alive that could paint that picture and something else, no artist's skill can ever bring out on a canvas that distance from the throne of God, that place of Glory, that place of the scepter and the crown, to the basin and the towel and the disciples feet!

No surveyor's chain could measure that distance. The only sword by which Christ could become the Captain of our salvation was in that towel.

Many a man can lift a crown and a throne, but cannot lift a towel.

What can we learn from this truth? That Jesus is giving us the example of becoming a servant. I cover this in great detail in my book, **"Give Me an Old Shoe."**

Chapter Five

WE MUST LEARN FROM HIS LABOR, John 13:4-5.

When Jesus rose from supper and wrapped that towel around His body and washed the feet of His disciples, He was performing an act of selfless service for His men. What Jesus did has a lot to teach us about becoming a people of the towel.

Several facts present themselves to us in these verses. **Washing feet was slaves' work.** Even Jewish servants could not be forced to wash their master's feet. It was a task reserved for the lowest of Gentile slaves. Sometimes, a child would wash a parent's feet; a wife would wash the feet of her husband; or a friend would wash a friend's feet in a display of extreme affection. So, Jesus took the place of a slave before His disciples. He willingly humbles Himself to meet a need in the lives of His men.

Jesus washed the feet of His disciples without being asked to do so. In fact, they were probably shocked when Jesus began to wash their feet, John 13:6, 8. It was a breach of hospitality to fail to wash a guest's feet, Luke 7:40-50.

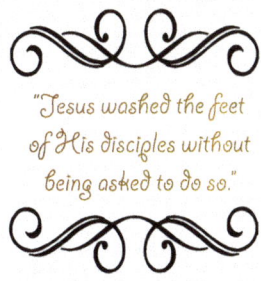

"Jesus washed the feet of His disciples without being asked to do so."

The disciples should have been falling all over one another to wash His feet, but it never entered their minds to serve Him. Apparently, they were all waiting for someone to serve them.

CREEPING BLACK MOLD

Just look at the lessons that Jesus taught them with His servant heart:

Jesus served with no expectation of reward. No one even said thank you. He did what He did just because He wanted to do it.

"Jesus served those with a willing heart."

Jesus served the others with a willing heart. No one had to twist His arm. He voluntarily took the place of a slave and served His men.

Jesus served those who did not deserve to be served. Think about it! He washed the feet of Simon Peter. Before the night would end those feet would stand at a Roman fire as Peter denied Jesus three times. Jesus also washed the feet of Judas Iscariot. His feet had already carried him to the Jewish leaders where he bargained away the life of Jesus for a few pieces of silver.

Before this night would end, those same feet would carry him back to the Jews where he would completely abandon Jesus to His enemies. Jesus washed the feet of the other ten and before the night would end, all of those feet would run away in fear. Jesus knew all of this, yet He served them all anyway.

When verse 5 says that Jesus **"began to wash ... and to wipe"** the feet of the disciples, both those verbs are in a

- 80 -

Chapter Five

tense that speaks of continual, ongoing activity. In other words, Jesus kept at the task until it was completed. He worked until every dirty foot had been cleansed.

How about you, how about me? How many times have we left the task that Jesus called us to do and never completed it due to fear, failure or just personal desires first?

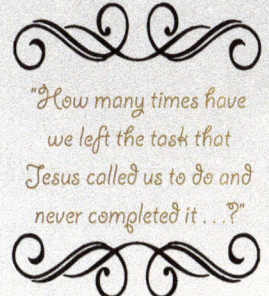

"How many times have we left the task that Jesus called us to do and never completed it...?"

Jesus did what He did for a very specific purpose. While He and His men were celebrating the Passover, the disciples were occupied with other matters. While they were in the upper room that night, Jesus was occupied with the weighty matters of eternity. He knew that before the night ended, He would go to Gethsemane where He would labor in prayer before His Father. He knew that Judas would betray Him to the Jews. He knew that the Romans would arrest Him and put Him on trial. He knew that before twenty-four hours would pass, He would be condemned, rejected by His people, beaten, crucified and buried.

He knew that He would bear the sins of His people on Calvary and die in their place. His mind carried all these burdens, still He wanted to serve His men.

While Jesus carried the burden of the lost on His heart, His men were worried about far more trivial matters. Luke 22:24-30

CREEPING BLACK MOLD

tells us that they were arguing about who should be the greatest among the disciples. Jesus used this opportunity to teach them what being a true servant was all about.

Most of us are like the disciples. There are very few who truly possess a servant's heart. Most are willing to be served, but not too many are willing to serve others. Like Jesus, we should be willing to serve others regardless of the cost.

We must be willing to humble ourselves and do whatever is necessary to serve others, Philippians 2:4; Romans 12:10. Someone has to do the grunt work!

"We must learn to serve without having to be asked."

We must learn to serve others willingly, with no thought of reward, Matthew 6:2-4. Whose praise would you rather have? Men or that of the Lord?

We must learn to serve those who are selfish and who refuse to serve.

Chapter Five

We must teach the next generation how to serve. Teach them by encouraging them to be more involved in service. Teach them by example!

There is much we can learn from our Lord's labor. He served others and set a standard for us that we should strive to reach in our own service. That is one step toward our becoming a people of the towel.

1. **We Must Learn From His Labor**
2. **We Must Learn From His Lordship**

Everything Jesus did that night reminds us of Who He is and what He came to this world to do. Let me run through a short list of facts that stands out.

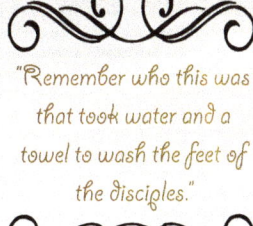
"Remember who this was that took water and a towel to wash the feet of the disciples."

I am just trying to remind you - Who this was that took water and a towel to wash the feet of the disciples.

> - This man was and is God in human flesh.
> - This was and is the Lord of glory.
> - This is the Creator of all things, Colossians 1:16.
> - This is God in human flesh, John 1:1, 14; Philippians 2:5-8; Colossians 1:15; John 14:9.

CREEPING BLACK MOLD

This is the Savior, Redeemer and Deliverer of lost sinners, I Peter 1:18-19. This is the King of Kings and the Lord of Lords, Revelation 19:16.

If the Lord Jesus Christ would condescend to serve the disciples; we have no excuse for not serving others. If He would wash the feet of Peter and Judas; how much more should we seek ways to serve those around us?

We are never more like Jesus than when we are serving others. In Luke 6:40, Jesus says, *"The disciple is not above his master: but every one that is perfect shall be as his master."* When we humble ourselves and assume the position of a slave before others, we demonstrate true Christ likeness. When we do, He is gloried and He will honor our service in His way for His glory, James 4:10; 1 Peter 5:5-6.

Serving others is a recipe for happiness. When we can come to the place where we stop worrying about who is doing what and we simply serve who we can where we can, we will live a more blessed Christian life. If we could ever come to the place where it does not matter who does what job; who gets the glory for what is done; or even why the task needs to be accomplished, we would be developing into a people of the towel.

1. **We Must Learn From His Labor**
2. **We Must Learn From His Lordship**

Chapter Five

By the way, a true servant looks at the needs around him and just does what needs to be done, without being asked; without expectation of reward; without expectation of thanks; with nothing more at heart than a desire to love and act like Jesus Christ. That is what defines the people of the towel.

Notice now with me:

II. **God's People Ought to have <u>Beautiful</u> feet.**

The relevance of this text that I am about to ask you to read with me, is huge for understanding how you came to be saved from God's wrath and from the guilt and dominion of sin with the hope of eternal joy in God. It is huge for understanding how your children or parents or brothers and sisters or neighbors or colleagues or the unreached peoples of the world will be saved. The process of coming to faith and salvation is laid out here as nowhere else.

Before you read the next passage of Scripture, we must recall what Paul had stressed that Jew and Gentile have no distinction in the enjoyment of the riches of God's glory. Both, with no distinction, will enjoy the fullness of God's salvation if they call on the name of the Lord.

Turn now to Romans 10:14-17 and you will find the steps themselves so that you know what you must do to be a part of God's saving plan for ourselves and our family and

CREEPING BLACK MOLD

friends and the nations without the gospel. Let's read verses 14-17.

When Paul says, *"How beautiful are the feet of those who preach good news,"* he is quoting Isaiah 52:7.

Bringers of Good News Are <u>Precious</u> and <u>Beautiful</u>.

➢ First, preachers of the gospel and those that are bringers of God's good news – are so precious that we see even their soiled and bloody feet as beautiful. Beautiful feet are not soft, manicured, painted, well-tanned feet.

➢ Beautiful feet are like the dirty, worn, wrinkled, leathery, scarred feet from many miles of trekking into remote places with good news that could not be heard any other way. So the first point of quoting Isaiah 52:7 is this: bringers of good news are precious people – people of whom the world is not worthy – beautiful for their worn out bodies in the service of King Jesus.

Paul Brand, the medical missionary to India, said that his missionary mother took all the mirrors out of her house when he told her at about age 70 she had aged; and for the last 20 years of her missionary life (into her nineties) she never had a mirror in the house in the mountains of India. When she died villages gathered from all through the mountains to bury a beautiful woman.

Chapter Five

God Has Sent People
- YOU AND I THAT ARE BORN AGAIN -
with the Good News, why not share it?

Here is a continuation of the chain of human responsibility. Here is stressed the need for a Divine commission. Certainly God calls some men to a full time ministry, and no one should assume the office of the ministry without a Divine call but He also calls every saved person to be His witnesses. For the most part, the Christians in our day has forsaken their responsibility to witness. It should be remembered that the commission of Matthew 28:19-20 was not delivered just to the clergy, but to the whole church and to understand this, we must remember that in Bible times travel was generally by foot over dusty roads, so that the feet of the messengers of the gospel would be the first things defiled, yet they are pronounced beautiful because of their mission. It might rather have been expected that the beauty of the lips speaking the message would have been stressed but such is not the case. The gospel is called *"peace"* because this is the consequence of it when it results in justification, Romans 5:1. Here is also a Biblical definition of the gospel: it is *"glad tidings of good things"* or good news, as the word literally means.

CREEPING BLACK MOLD

Our responsibility is to declare the Lord's message faithfully, and to leave the results to the Lord. We have been faithful and successful when we do so. If the hearers refuse to believe the message, that is their responsibility, and they must be prepared to answer for rejecting it, Ezekiel 2:3-7. God must not only empower the message, but He must also fit the hearer to receive the message.

Power alone is not enough, for how bright must the light be for a man to see it if he has no eyes? God has commanded that the gospel be preached universally, but He has also declared that there will be only a limited success to it. This is all a part of His eternal purpose of grace. Grace is always distinguishing and this would not be so if all responded to the message of grace, and fallen man would assume that salvation were a right, and that God owed it to man.

Romans 10:17 says, "So then faith cometh by hearing, and hearing by the word of God."

Here is how God works faith in man — by the instrumentality of the Word of God and the Holy Spirit. What then can be said of the person who absolutely refuses to read or hear the Word? He cuts himself off from the possibility of believing, and so from the hope of salvation. This is the only way one can get faith, without which it is impossible to please God, Hebrews 11:6. *"Hearing"* here is the same Greek word rendered *"report"* in Romans 10:16, and the reference is to

Chapter Five

Isaiah's description of the suffering Messiah, so that saving faith comes only where the gospel has been preached.

Do you have beautiful feet?

III. **God's People Ought to have "PREPARED FEET," Ephesians 6:15.**

This book is not about me to come with a rod, but a book where I come with a deep longing for myself and with a happy dream of what it might be like if God would make us a healthier, happy, free, authentic, loving, powerful, evangelistic, outreaching Christian.

Now what does Ephesians 6:15 (NKJV) say to us? ***"Having shod your feet with the PREPARATION (READINESS) OF THE GOSPEL OF PEACE."***

"The Gospel of Peace"

Before we focus on the word *"preparation"* and its place in the armor of God, I want to say just a word about the *"gospel of peace."*

The gospel that we have for the world - the gospel that we have is the good news that God purchased peace by the death of his Son Jesus Christ and offers it to all sinners who believe in Jesus Christ.

CREEPING BLACK MOLD

We have the good news that God's omnipotent wrath against sinners has been taken away through the death of Jesus for sin. Everyone who believes is reconciled to him freely by grace, and in the place of enmity comes peace. There is nothing sweeter in the entire world than to be at peace with God.

Look at Ephesians 2:13-18 to see how Paul, under the leadership of the Holy Spirit, developed the gospel of peace for us.

The good news of peace is that when Christ died and shed his blood for sin, two kinds of enmity were overcome. The enmity between God and repentant sinners was brought to an end, and the enmity between races and factions in Christ was brought to an end. So Christ became our peace. That is the *"gospel of peace."*

We have heard it by the grace of God. We have believed it by the grace of God, and we have been saved through it by the grace of God. Now Paul says in Ephesians 6:15 that the preparation (readiness) of this *"gospel of peace"* is to be put on like shoes as part of our spiritual armor. *". . . and having shod your feet with the preparation (readiness) of the gospel of peace."*

So let's think for a few minutes about this preparation (readiness) as part of the whole armor of God. Verses 11–12 say, *"Put on the whole armor of God, that you may be able to stand against the wiles of the devil. For we wrestle not (are*

Chapter Five

not contending) against flesh and blood, but against principalities, against powers, against the rulers of the darkness of this world (the world rulers of this present darkness), against (the) spiritual (hosts of) wickedness in high (heavenly) places."

The Purpose of Having Our Feet Shod

Let me address four things that we learn from those two verses in Ephesians 2:11-12

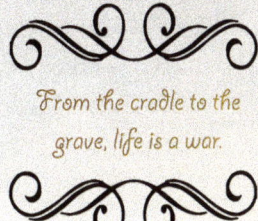

From the cradle to the grave, life is a war.

1. **All <u>Life</u> Is War**

   From the cradle to the grave, life is a war. Your soul, your mind, your body, your family, your career are fields of conflict. Until Satan is finally thrown into the lake of fire, our peace with God will have to be a vigilant peace because Satan will certainly give us no peace if we are at peace with God.

2. **The War Is Against <u>Supernatural</u> Evil Powers**

   The war we are in is not a war with flesh and blood but with supernatural evil powers. What amazes me about Paul's words here is not what he affirms but what he denies. I'm not surprised to hear him say that we wrestle with evil angelic, demonic, supernatural powers. What surprises me is that he says in Ephesians 6:12 *"we do **NOT** wrestle with flesh and blood."*

CREEPING BLACK MOLD

I think Paul would answer, *"You're right. Flesh and blood is real and it can be very evil, but what I mean is this. Whenever someone's flesh attacks me, or someone's blood boils against me, or my way is hindered by man, something else is also going on, something deeper, bigger, more terrible, more sinister, and more destructive than meets the eye. I don't mean that flesh and blood can't hurt or hinder the cause of Christ. I mean that the prince of the power of the air is more dangerous than any of his subjects and that he must be overcome in every instance of conflict or the battle is lost."*

For a moment think of Ephesians 2:1–2 (NKJV). *"And you He made alive, who were dead in trespasses and sins, in which you once walked according to the course of this world, according to the prince of the power of the air, the spirit who now works in the sons of disobedience."*

Sure, the sons of disobedience (in their flesh and blood reality) can oppose us in our spiritual warfare; but it's more decisive to defeat the spirit that works in them and the prince of the power of the air that they follow, than simply to wrestle as though all you are dealing with is human nature.

So the first thing we see in Ephesians 6:11–12 is that life is war, and the second thing we see is that the conflict, if it is going to be successful, will be fought with supernatural or demonic forces. If they are not engaged, the victory is superficial.

3.   **There Is Danger of <u>Falling</u> in This Battle**

Chapter Five

Believe it or not, there is danger of falling in this battle. Three times Paul tells us to take pains to stand, that is, not to fall. Why not spend some time on this issue of perseverance in the book of Hebrews for a great understanding of this subject of perseverance.

4. **God Has Made Provision for Us to <u>Stand</u> and not <u>fall</u>**

God is able to keep us from falling, as Jude says in verse 24, and the way he keeps us from falling **is by fitting us for successful spiritual combat**. So if your aim is to persevere in the Christian life and not be defeated by the wiles of the devil, then you must put on the armor described in these verses. This is how God means to keep us safe unto the day of salvation.

Having Our Feet Shod with "Readiness"

That's the context in which we read about having our feet shod with the readiness of the gospel of peace (verse 15). Notice that we are not shod with the gospel. The gospel is the Word of God and the Word of God is our sword according to verse 17. We are not shod with the gospel. What we are shod with is the READINESS of the gospel. Now what does that mean?

Feet Shod with "Readiness" - Ready to Move with the Gospel - Experience the Power of the Gospel.

Ready to Move with the Gospel

CREEPING BLACK MOLD

I think it means, "Let your feet be ready to move with the gospel." Feet are for moving from one place to another. If you put on shoes of readiness, then the idea would seem to be ready to do what feet are for, namely, moving. If the readiness is readiness of the gospel, it probably means ready to move with the gospel—move with gospel power and for gospel purposes.

A Parallel in I Peter 3:15

One last confirmation: In I Peter 3:15 (NKJV) the very word *"ready"* is used in the same kind of exhortation. *"Always be ready to give (make) a defense to everyone (anyone) who asks (calls) you a reason (to account) for the hope that is in you, with meekness and fear (yet do it with gentleness and reverence)."*

Experiencing the Power of the Gospel

So, coming back to Ephesians 6:15 (NKJV), I have one last observation. The armor of God is given to us believers to stand against the devil. It is introduced as defensive armor. In verse 13 we read, *"Take the whole armor of God that you may be able to withstand in the evil day, and having done all, to stand."* How to stay standing is the issue.

So what can we conclude from the fact that the shoes of verse 15 are the readiness to move with the gospel of peace? A ready offense is an essential part of a successful defense. Oh how true this is!

Chapter Five

Giving the gospel away is one of the best ways of experiencing its power in your own life. The best way to taste the power of God for your own soul is to venture something on it. It's the great old truth of the Lord himself when he said, *"He who loses his life for my sake and the gospel's will save it."* The more ready we are to move with the gospel, the more life and power and joy and security we will know in the gospel.

In giving we will receive. In dying we will live. In telling the gospel we will hear it again with so much more depth and power and joy.

*How lovely on the mountains are the feet of
him who brings good news,
good news proclaiming peace,
announcing news of happiness:
Our God reigns! Our God reigns!*

CREEPING BLACK MOLD

WHAT KIND OF FEET DO YOU HAVE?

Chapter Five

THOUGHTS:

_____
_____
_____
_____
_____
_____
_____
_____
_____
_____

ACTIONS:

_____
_____
_____
_____
_____
_____
_____
_____
_____
_____

CHAPTER SIX

SIN #5 - "A WICKED HEART"

Chapter Six

Proverbs 6:18 says, **"An heart that deviseth wicked imaginations…"**

<u>Let's take the word, *"wicked"* for a moment</u>. It will be understood, that by the wicked, we here intend careless, unawakened sinners.

Then why is this heart wicked?

The wicked does not seek after God. The expression implies, not only that they do not seek after him, but that the wicked will not. It is the settled, determined purpose of their hearts, not to seek him; and to this purpose they will stubbornly and unalterably adhere, unless their wills are convicted by the Holy Spirits voice.

The wicked does not seek after the likeness of God nor do they, not at all, resemble God. These folks do not desire or endeavor

CREEPING BLACK MOLD

to resemble any of His love towards one of His own, therefore, in their view, no reason why they should. One has said, *"There are but two motives, which can induce any being to imitate another, or to wish to resemble him. The first is a wish to obtain the approbation of the person imitated. The second is admiration of something in his character, and a consequent desire to inscribe it into our own."* But the wicked can be influenced by neither of these motives to seek after conformity to God. They cannot be led to imitate him by a wish to obtain his favor; for this, as we have already seen, they have no desire to obtain, so then, since they have no wish to imitate their Savior, they cannot, they will not seek to walk after Christ.

I like what Oswald Chambers said in his notes on Jeremiah. *"Jeremiah is not suffering for his own sin, or because he is sensitive; he is suffering because he has seen what God knew better than anyone, that there is a deep moral tragedy at the heart of human beings. Sin is not weakness, it is not disease, it is red-handed rebellion against God, and the magnitude of that rebellion is expressed in the Cross of Christ."* Then in Jeremiah 17:9 we find these words, *"the heart is deceitful above all things, and desperately wicked: who can know it."*

As a Christian, there is one that we all need to work on and it is the word *"vengeance."* This word is the root of *"a wicked and deceitful heart,"* in my opinion. Let me explain it this way.

Vengeance is the deepest-rooted passions in the human heart. There is no other word as deep as this word. The devil hates God and His saints, those born again by the blood of Christ, if sin has not

Chapter Six

reached you in its awful heights; it may well do so unless we let God alter the guidance of our hearts. That is why the verse in Proverbs 6:18, gives us such a heed warning with so much attention to not have a **"heart that manufactures wicked plans."**

It is great to know that God does change the heart and when His new life is in our hearts, we can work it out through our head and express it in our lives.

Now, let's turn our thoughts to James 1:26. *"If any man among you seem to be religious, and bridleth not his tongue, but deceiveth his own heart, this man's religion is vain."*

Now, the fault referred to, and the disposition supposed in precepts and reflections concerning the government of the tongue, is not evil speaking from malice, nor lying of bearing false witness from indirect selfish designs. The disposition to these and the actual vices themselves all come under other subjects. The tongue may be employed about, and made to serve all the purposes of the vices, in tempting and deceiving, and injustice. But, the thing here supposed and referred to is talkativeness; a disposition to be talking, abstracted from the consideration of what is to be said; with very little or no regard to, or thought of doing, either good, or harm. So then, as a Christian to imagine this to be a slight matter, and that it deserves not to have so great weight laid upon it, we have to consider what evil is implied in it, and the bad effects which follow from it. The thing is, to engage your attention; to take you up wholly for the present time: what reflections will be made afterwards is in truth the least of their thoughts. Further, when persons, who indulge themselves in these

CREEPING BLACK MOLD

liberties of the tongue, are in any degree offended with another, as little disgusts and misunderstandings will be, they allow themselves to defame and revile such a one without any moderation or bounds; though the offence is so very slight, that they themselves would, not do, nor perhaps wish, him an injury in any other way. To put it another way, if a Christian, from deep malice and desire of revenge, should meditate a falsehood, with a settled design to ruin his neighbor's reputation, and should, with great coolness and deliberation, spread it, nobody would choose to say of such a one, that he had no government of his tongue. Here the crime is injustice and perjury; and, strictly speaking, no more belongs to the present subject, than perjury and injustice in any other way. But there is such a thing as a disposition to be talking for its own sake; from which persons often say anything, good or bad, of others, merely as a subject of discourse, according to the particular temper or mood they themselves happen to be in, and to pass away the present time under the influence of Satan. There is likewise to be observed in persons, such a strong and eager desire of engaging attention to what they say, that they will speak good or evil, truth or otherwise, merely as one or the other seems to be most hearkened to: and this, though it is sometimes joined, is not the same with the desire of being thought important and men of consequence. There is in some such a disposition to be talking, that an offence of the slightest kind, and such as would not raise any other resentment, yet raises, if I may so speak, the resentment of the tongue, puts it into a flame, into the most ungovernable motions. The tongue, used in such a devious manner, does a world of mischief; and implies not only great folly, and a trifling spirit, but great viciousness of mind, great indifference to truth, and to the reputation, welfare, and good of others. So much reason is there for what James 3:6 says of the tongue, *"It is*

Chapter Six

a fire, a world of iniquity; it defileth the whole body, and setteth on fire the course of nature; and it is set on fire of hell." This is the faculty or disposition which we are required to keep a guard upon; these are the vices and follies it runs into when not kept under due restraint.

As to the government of the tongue, in respect to talking upon indifferent subjects: After what has been said concerning the due government of it in respect to the occasions and times for silence, there is little more necessary, than only to caution men to be fully satisfied, that the subjects are indeed of an indifferent nature; and not to spend too much time in conversation of this kind. But persons must be sure to take heed, that the subject of their conversation be at least of an indifferent nature: that it is in no way offensive to virtue, religion, reputation or good manners; that it is not of a hateful, dissolute sort, this leaving always ill impressions upon the mind; that it in no way is injurious to others reputations.

I know that I am spending more time on this subject, but; it is because of the harm one can do not only to the Christian brother or sister, but to the winning of the unsaved that is seeking Christ and seeing Christ in a professing Christian at work or in the church.

I like this story told by Gene Getz: *"a farmer's wife who had spread a slanderous story about another Christian in the village in which she lived. Soon the whole countryside had heard it. Sometime later the woman became sick and confessed the story was untrue. After her recovery she came to the person she had slandered and asked his pardon. The Christian responded, 'Of course I will pardon you, if you will comply with a wish of mine.'*

CREEPING BLACK MOLD

'Gladly,' replied the woman.

'Go home then,' said the Christian, 'kill a black hen, pluck the feathers, and put them in a basket and bring them here.' In half an hour the woman was back. 'Now,' said the Christian, 'go through the village and at each street corner scatter a few of these feathers. Then take the remaining ones to the top of the bell tower of the church and scatter them to the winds.' She did so, and when she returned the Christian said, 'Now go through the village and gather the feathers again, and see that not one is missing.'

The woman looked at the Christian in astonishment and said, 'Why that is impossible, the wind has scattered them over the fields everywhere!'

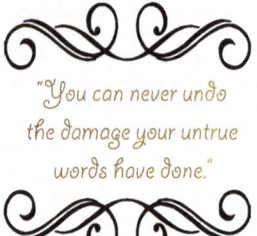

"You can never undo the damage your untrue words have done."

'And so' said the Christian, 'while I forgive you gladly, do not forget that you can never undo the damage your untrue words have done.'"

Yes, God forgives and so do people that have been hurt, but there are some things that you or myself can do or say that can never be undone completely. Yes, the scars may last for a lifetime.

Before you go on to the next point, stop and think if you are guilty of such a travesty to another Christian or unsaved person that can and will hurt the cause of Christ as well and hinder their walk with or decision for Christ.

- 104 -

Chapter Six

Why not calls, text, better yet, go and visit them and ask for forgiveness.

Secondly, let's look at the word "imaginations." It comes from the noun *"chashab"* that means to *"plan, make judgment, to invent; its part form indicates a weaver. The principle idea is that of using the mind in the activity of thinking, creating new ideas"* (Definitions of Lexical Aids to the Old Testament, Edited by Spiros Zodhites, THD). In this verse it means, from this definition and its Hebrew word, *"contrivance, cunning works."*

The description of the heart here exactly corresponds with the condition of most men at the time of the flood, and which was the cause of it, (Genesis 6:5-7). **"The heart (not merely evil, as all men's hearts are naturally) but, deliberately and continually, of set purpose, <u>devising wicked imaginations</u> is set the middle of the seven abominations, for it is the center whence the rest emanate,"** (Faussett). The heart is the fountain while the feet carry out the thoughts of the heart, like a stream carries out the waters of the fountain. *"The eagerness and industry of sinners in their sinful pursuits, may shame us who go about that which is good so awkwardly and so coldly,"* (M. Henry).

CREEPING BLACK MOLD

"If any man among you seem to be religious, and bridleth not his tongue, but deceiveth his own heart, this man's religion is vain."

Chapter Six

THOUGHTS:
_____
_____
_____
_____
_____
_____
_____
_____
_____
_____
_____

ACTIONS:
_____
_____
_____
_____
_____
_____
_____
_____
_____
_____
_____

CHAPTER SEVEN

SIN #6 — "BEARING FALSE WITNESS"

Chapter Seven

Few people realize the awesome, destructive power of the human tongue. Because of a misspoken word, homes, friendships and churches have been splintered, destroyed, reputations shattered and lives literally destroyed and even ended. Proverbs 6:19 deals primarily with one's testimony in a trial setting and God says that we must never be guilty of lying on our neighbor or fellow Christian thereby causing him to suffer. We are exhorted to always be truthful and absolutely honest when dealing with another person. As we consider some of what God has said about the tongue, may God help us to understand that every time we speak of another, we literally hold that person's reputation and future in our hand!

Let me preface this study with two statements:

1. **A False Witness will use harsh words that only hurt and are meant to wound and inflict pain.**

CREEPING BLACK MOLD

A False Testimony is unnecessary not only in the Christian realm, but in the secular world as well. *"Let your speech be always with grace, seasoned with salt, that ye may know how ye ought to answer every man"* (Colossians 4:6). Did you get that message? Some years ago, Chinese Christians engaged in a form of witness which they called *"gossiping the Gospel"* - just talking quite naturally about **CHRIST** and His things in the way of ordinary conversation. A very commendable form of speech for **GOD**, don't you think? In the book of James we are warned of the ill that our tongues can bring into other lives, yet how great the blessings they can bring. That is a remarkable claim made by the ungodly, in Psalm 12:4, *"Our lips are our own, who is lord over us?"* No Christian should ever say that! **CHRIST** is Lord over us, our lips are not our own – nothing of ours is ours. Paul said, *"Ye are not your own…."* (I Corinthians 6:19). Mind, mouth, and members belong to Him who bought us. May our lips, then, be used always for good and for **GOD**.

We do not forget that GOD hears what we say.

- Sometimes it is what distresses Him, *"He hath heard your murmurings"* (Exodus 16:9).

- Sometimes it is what delights Him, *"Then they that feared the Lord spake often one to another, and the Lord hearkened*

Chapter Seven

and heard it, and a book of remembrance was written before Him for them that feared the Lord, and that thought upon His Name" (Malachi 3:16).

That **"hearkened"** is noteworthy, as if to indicate, speaking humanly, that He not only heard, but, as it were, cupped His ear to catch it all.

In the first case, He had to listen; in the second case, He wanted to listen. Let us then, sometimes, as opportunity affords, engage our tongues, to believers or to unbelievers, to talk tactfully about the One who means everything to us.

"Salt." Pungency sometimes, yes, when dealing with corrupt things. But graciousness always, as characterized the Master's conversation – "Never man spake like this Man," (John 7:46). If we be *"in Christ,"* if He be in us, should we not catch something of His tone and accent?

Would not this mean that, no repetition of slander, no suspicion of uncleanness, no temper, no criticism of others, no giving as much as we get, no undue exaggeration, not even slight variation from the truth, no unkind word ever? Verily, *"if any man offend not in word, the same is a perfect man"* (James 3:2) - that is, a man of full stature in **CHRIST**. May we always say as the Psalmist, *"Set a watch, O Lord, before my mouth; keep the door of my lips"* (Psalm 141:3).

CREEPING BLACK MOLD

I think that our passage has one more thing to say about the Christian ministry of the tongue.

Colossians 4:6 - "That ye may know how ye ought to answer every man."

We link this up with a later passage, *"Be ready always to give an answer to every man that asketh you a reason of the hope that is in you, with meekness and fear"* (I Peter 3:15).

The last part of this verse corresponds to the **"how"** of our Colossians verse. When we are trying to explain to another the reasonableness of our belief there is a proper way to do it, a true Christian spirit in which to talk.

One has said, *"Almost as important as knowing what to say is to **'know how'** to say it."* Like our ordinary conversation, this also is to be **"always with grace, seasoned with salt."** At the very beginning of the early Christian Church we are told of the two great characteristics of the apostles' **"witness"** - which should qualify both our public and our private testimony – **"great power. . . and great grace."**

Then, shall we not ask for strength of conviction, and sweetness of manner? Well now, if our **"answer,"** our **"reason,"** is to be intelligent, and in any degree effective, it will need careful and constant study. Should we not make it our aim to get a firm grasp of the meaning and teaching of the doctrine?

Chapter Seven

To get a growing, and deepening knowledge of it will surely be the ambition of us all, if it is to be to us, among many other things, *"the Sword of the Spirit"* (Ephesians 6:17). We must learn to use it effectively by constant sword drill. That will come, not by reading a few verses in the morning – even though that is an excellent preparation for the day - but by earnest and diligent study of the Word of **GOD's** dealings, and purposes of love for men and apply it daily in our walk with Him before others.

Surely this will bring the **"grace"** into our **"answer"** not only the **Book** knowledge, but the **Look** acquaintance of Isaiah.

2.   A False Witness brings self-destruction.

Take time now to turn to Proverbs 6:19; 12:17; 14:5; 19:5; 21:28 and spend some time there. Think on these things! Then you will find that the only way that a Christian can walk after God is by not bearing a false witness.

Will you agree with me that today we live in a *"not so truthful society?"* For example, leaders in government, business, education and yes even in the ministry of *"religion"* knowingly lie numerous times each day and think nothing of it especially if it is for their benefit. They are not alone in the practice. Most people admit that they lie often. Straying from the truth is an accepted *way of living*. Many think there are good—meaning that *little white*—and bad lies. Some would

CREEPING BLACK MOLD

never consider lying in a court of law, **yet many do**, but feel no remorse at giving false information on a job application. Some people believe that lying is necessary to keep things running smoothly—international relations, businesses, marriages and friendships.

What is the truth about lying? Is there good and bad lying? Do "little white lies" help or *hurt* people? Can stretching the truth and distorting the facts cause considerable damage to individuals and whole nations? The plain truth is revealing.

Our world today is constantly being flooded with all kinds of untruths and the children are quickly picking up on this as a part of their everyday lives. Self-deception, spiritual hypocrisy and false religious instruction are reaching pandemic proportions. As you study prophecy you will quickly find that this world is quickly heading into its worst crisis ever. It is an event so terrifying that Jesus Christ warned His disciples about the soon-coming Great Tribulation. He said that religious deception would be the leading cause of the crisis at the close of man's rule on earth (Matthew 24:4-5). As individuals, we must be sure that we fully understand the critical importance of the passage of Scripture and what it can to do to others as well as one.

With incredible power, God spoke from Mount Sinai, *"Thou shalt not bear false witness against thy neighbor"* (Exodus 20:16). Let's look at this briefly. A fifth of the commandments related to preserving loving relationships among

Chapter Seven

mankind. Remember, the first four commandments show us how to love God; the last six explain how to love other humans. Besides preserving the family structure, marriage, human life and other human beings' possessions, with the Ninth Commandment, God seeks to guard what is next most important to any human: his reputation. This commandment forbids all lying, which includes the sins of slander and gossip. A thief takes physical things that are easily replaced; however, a man's reputation taken by lies, slander or gossip is often never restored. As a pastor for over fifty years I have seen this happen so many times and one that has been hurt by lies or gossip never returns to church.

God gave us this advice to show us that all men, women and children must control their tongues.

How true what James says about the tongue in James 3:5. It was Guy H. King that said of the tongue, *"A subject that is in everybody's mouth."* The human tongue is a tiny organ, yet it wields incredible power. The Apostle James wrote, *"Behold also the ships, which though they be so great, and are driven of fierce winds, yet are they turned about with a very small helm, whithersoever the governor listeth. Even so the tongue is a little member…"* (James 3:4-5).

Here the tongue is compared to the rudder of a large ship. Though it is the smallest part of the vessel, it has the power to direct its course. All too often, the power unleashed by the human tongue is a destructive one. James continued, *"Behold, how great a matter a little fire kindleth! And the tongue is a fire, a world of iniquity: so is the tongue among our members, that it defileth the whole body, and setteth on fire the course of nature; and it is set on fire of hell"* (verses 5-6).

Over five times James brings us this subject. It was Matthew Henry that called these, *"tongue sins."* I wonder how James would look upon the church today if he came for a visit for just a few weeks.

Let's take some time here to see how James approaches this subject and the illustrations he is led by the Holy Spirit to use. With great wealth of his imaginations, James illustrates for us the power of the tongue over the rest of the body.

1.   **The Bridle and the Horse, James 3:2b-3.**

We are told in chapter one and verse twenty six of James that the man who does control his tongue is able to bridle the whole body as well. I believe that he is saying that the spirit of the Christian does not go out of the man but the restless energy of that Christian is under control and guidance. It certainly does not mean that a man or woman that is saved should be dumb and lifeless, without ambition and power, but simply that his tongue, like the rest of his body, should be kept in control. In Psalm 39:1, David said, *"I will take heed to my ways that I sin not with my tongue: I will keep my mouth with a bridle."*

Chapter Seven

The horse has to follow his mouth, in which the bridle is placed. The purpose of the bridle is that the horses may obey the rider and it is thoroughly successful, as a rule. So we should place bridles in our mouths for the deliberate purpose of controlling the tongue. It will not happen by accident. If the bridle is good for the horse, it is far more so for the man or woman as the case may be.

2. **The Rudder and the Ship, James 3:4.**

Great as the ship may be, the silent forces of nature are still greater. Man has not yet mastered all the powers of nature. But the ship, blind to its fate, responds to the will of the steersman. The lesson is very clear, one must watch the tongue if he is to avoid shipwreck.

I could go on, but I will let you finish verses five through twelve, I will conclude with this thought: James exaggerates the evil of the tongue. The crisp wisdom of James about the tongue makes one wonder afresh if his mother had not taught him some of the aphorisms as a child.

Don't be like Peter in his hour of failure, resented it; if by the manner of our speech, and by the use of our tongue we may gladly welcome it, if by the manner of our speech, and by the use of our tongue, we betray ourselves to the world **as one of His**.

CREEPING BLACK MOLD

When we deeply meditate on these verses, we realize that there has been untold human suffering and damage caused by people who carelessly lie, slander or gossip about another human being. Yet all parties are damaged by such actions. Who can ever trust a liar, slanderer or gossiper? The Proverbs state, *"He that hideth hatred with lying lips, and he that uttereth a slander, is a fool"* Proverbs 10:18. Why? *"Death and life are in the power of the tongue: and they that love it shall eat the fruit thereof"* (Proverbs 18:21). Dear friend, lying causes great harm to *all* involved, so let's be careful.

Follow me now a little further. Let's look at: The Damage of destroying a reputation.

The simple application of this verse is to not give false testimony in a legal setting. To lie in a court of law is called perjury. Serious penalties are imposed in many countries for committing such an act. It is right to do so. Why? Our judicial system is based on truth. The sad fact is, many commit the crime of perjury every day. Some government leaders, educators, business people, men and women think nothing of lying on a witness stand. What makes their sin even more shocking is the fact that they attempt to deceive the judge and jury by *swearing to tell the truth*—putting their right hand on the Bible and invoking the name of God. Such poor conduct is a monstrous lie in itself. It says much about the lack of real morals in our society.

Surely we can understand what an outrage this is to the great God, whose word is *truth* (John 17:17).

Chapter Seven

All one has to do today is to look at the news, see it on your Iphone or Ipad, how the crime of perjury runs rampant through all levels of our society—from the very top to the bottom. We should not forget that a former president of our nation lied openly to the Senate and congressional committees. Yet, he was not removed from office. Think about the message this sad fact sent to the rest of the world. Are we a nation that is OK with lies, deception and hypocrisy?

The damage caused by false testimony is enormous. No one trusts a known enemy. Our criminal lying shows us that we cannot even trust our elected officials, friends, spouses, business partners, work associates and sad to say, pastors or anyone that has been called to preach or teach the gospel. Anyone who is familiar with our legal system knows that there is no such thing as a simple, inexpensive trial. Countless hours and millions of dollars are wasted checking out the truthfulness of witnesses. Why? People cannot be trusted to tell the truth.

Just think of the personal damage to people that regularly takes place because of false testimony. Bitter divorce and custody disputes can leave husband, wife and children scarred for life. It has been known that many will manufacture the worst false accusations to get custody, money and possessions. Just look at the example in Mark 14:56-63 of Jesus Christ, He was executed because of false witnesses.

CREEPING BLACK MOLD

To stop lying, we must understand why human beings lie. Study little children. Why do they lie? Generally, little children lie to *avoid punishment* or to *appear better than their peers*. With adults it is not any different. The root cause of this horrible sin is *vanity*.

Men and women lie because they are more concerned with the self than anything else. What is best for another human being is rarely considered. Many fear to speak the truth because they are obsessed with what others think about them. Yet, few people are concerned by what God thinks. This is especially true in the spheres of higher education and religion. The Apostle John said this about the religious leaders of his day: *"For they loved the praise of men more than the praise of God"* (John 12:43).

Lying may appear to be the best route to take in the short run. However, real lasting benefits can only come by recognizing and telling the truth.

Why do human beings so easily succumb to such a disgraceful habit?

It is not intellectually fashionable to believe that Satan the devil exists. He does! Our lying society is a major proof of this fact. Satan, the devil, is the author of all lying and deception.

John the apostle records Jesus Christ's own words revealing the truth about Satan. Upbraiding the religious leaders of His day, Christ said, *"Ye are of your father the devil, and the lusts of your father ye will do. He was a murderer from the beginning, and abode not in*

Chapter Seven

the truth, because there is no truth in him. When he speaketh a lie, he speaketh of his own: for he is a liar, and the father of it" (John 8:44). Here Christ shows that it was Satan who lied to our first parents, who told them they had an immortal soul—essentially murdering them. God had told them that if they rebelled against Him and walked the opposite way of His government, they surely would die (Genesis 2:16-17). Satan appealed to Eve's vanity, and she disobeyed God. Adam willingly followed his wife. They believed and followed a liar. They and the rest of mankind have suffered since.

Satan is a powerful angelic being that broadcasts—all over the earth—a spirit of disobedience, which includes lying and deception (Ephesians 2:2). It is Satan who tempts all humans to lie.

To be a Christian, an individual must believe what Christ says and strive to live as He lived.

In our personal lives, we must make sure that our words are always true. If we remain in the habit of lying to others and to ourselves, we will destroy our character and pervert and twist our own minds. Keeping our minds free of lies opens up an incredible clarity of thinking—the kind of thinking that cultivates deeper understanding of all truth.

Paul said it best when he taught, *"Wherefore putting away lying, speak every man truth with his neighbor: for we are members one of another"* (Ephesians 4:25). When we speak, let it always be the truth. However, this does not mean that we always have to reveal all that we know. In speaking the truth, we must always use wisdom, tact

CREEPING BLACK MOLD

and especially love. God's ministers are required to always speak the truth in love (verse 15). Sometimes the truth does hurt temporarily, but in the long run it is the best healing agent we could desire.

All men are only as good as their word. If we are habitual liars, none can trust us. What is worse, we cannot be helped spiritually. Who can help a liar? The clearest example of what we mean here is Satan the devil. Not even God can help him—his mind is permanently twisted.

Satan's character is diametrically opposite than that of God. If we choose to live as Satan lives, we will suffer a fearful fate. John records in Revelation: *"But the fearful, and unbelieving, and the abominable, and murderers, and whoremongers, and sorcerers, and idolaters, and all liars, shall have their part in the lake which burneth with fire and brimstone: which is the second death"* (Revelation 21:8). All humans who embrace the way of lying are in danger of being thrown into the lake of fire, which represents the ultimate punishment—eternal death.

Remember, there are no good lies in God's sight. Half-truths, distortions and deceptions are condemned throughout the Bible. Let's all learn to live and speak the truth and thereby inherit the glorious Kingdom of God.

Bottom line is this, according to God's Word, "if the truth cannot be told or received then let the lips be silent." Listen, **if our Savior can be discrete**, so can the saints!

Chapter Seven

As I close this chapter and this sin; let me share with you that:

YOUR REPUTATION IS A <u>VALUABLE POSSESSION</u>

- ➤ **According to the Bible**, one's *"good name,"* or reputation, is far more valuable than riches or expensive ointments, Proverbs 22:1. My dad, who is now in Heaven, told me when I was a small boy and we didn't have much, *"Son, all I can give you is a good name."*

- ➤ **Your Reputation Determines the Level of Respect You Receive** - No one puts much confidence in a person who is dishonest, deceptive, or otherwise living his life in a sinful, shameful manner. I really respect people about whom I never hear a negative remark. Jesus was such a man (Luke 2:52). We should do all that is in our power to see that we never allow our names to be associated with that which is disrespectful and shameful. It will undermine your good name and cause people to lose respect for you. Your life ought to be a beacon of integrity and decency.

- ➤ **Your Own Reputation is Valuable** - Therefore, guard it with your very life, and pray that others will do the same. Now, you cannot be responsible for what others do with your reputation, but you are responsible for what you do with theirs.

CREEPING BLACK MOLD

Your Reputation can be Vandalized Publicly.

It Is A Serious Thing - When we undermine the reputation of another by the words we speak, we are guilty of destroying that person's respectability and credibility before others. We are guilty of doing unspeakable damage to a person's life and ministry by the words we say about them.

I once read where a pastor was having trouble with a gossiper in the church. Every time she would see his car parked anywhere strange, she began immediately to spread the word that their pastor was having an affair. There was no truth to her rumors, but she kept it up until the pastor, in an effort to stop her mouth, left his car parked in front of her house, day and night for a week. That cured the problem!

CHAPTER SEVEN

Remember,
There are NO Good
Lies in
GOD's Sight.

CREEPING BLACK MOLD

THOUGHTS:

Chapter Seven

ACTIONS:

_____

_____

_____

_____

_____

_____

_____

_____

_____

_____

_____

_____

CHAPTER EIGHT

SIN #7 – "THE DANGER OF SOWING DISCORD!"

Chapter Eight

Let's try to imagine the following vivid scene: Here's the picture. Down front stands the groom in a spotless tuxedo - handsome, smiling, full of anticipation, shoes shined, every hair in place, anxiously awaiting the presence of his bride. All attendants are in place, looking joyful and attractive. The magical moment finally arrives as the pipe organ reaches full crescendo and the stately wedding march begins. Everyone rises and looks toward the door for their first glimpse of the bride but as they do there is a horrified gasp. The entire wedding party is shocked. The groom stares in an embarrassing disbelief - for, instead of a lovely woman dressed in elegant white, smiling behind a lace veil, the bride is LIMPING down the aisle. Her dress is SOILED and TORN. Her leg seems TWISTED. Ugly CUTS and BRUISES cover her bare arms. Her nose is BLEEDING, one eye is PURPLE and SWOLLEN, and her hair is DISHEVELED. Then you ask, *"Does not this handsome Groom deserve BETTER than this?"*

CREEPING BLACK MOLD

And then she gives us the clincher as she says: *"Alas, His bride, THE CHURCH has been fighting again."*

Well this is an accurate illustration of far too many congregations. In fact, the prevalence of dissension like this in the church led one unknown believer to say, *"To live above with those we love, oh how that will be glory. To live below with those we know...now that's another story."*

One of the greatest challenges that face any local church is the keeping the peace among the people. It has been said that when two Baptist get together there are three opinions presented.

It has always been the case even since the first century where the believers wrestled with personal relationships. Sometimes those tensions became so great that physical separation took place; for instance, in Acts 15:36-40, we find where Paul and Barnabas broke fellowship over a young man named John Mark.

Unfortunately Christians can and do hurt one another. Sometimes the pain is inflicted without malicious intent, but the agony is still the same. Why does this happen? Well I believe it is because of one word, *"FEAR!"*

- ➢ Fear of losing people
- ➢ Fear of not being liked
- ➢ Fear of losing financial resources
- ➢ Fear of being considered unloved
- ➢ Fear of confrontation

Chapter Eight

- Fear of appearing foolish YET
- **FEAR CAN PARALYZE THE VOICE**
- **FEAR CAN REDIRECT ONE'S THINKING TO CALL WRONG RIGHT!**

Turn to Galatians 2:14 and see what Paul did to Peter. **Peter was guilty of sowing discord among the Brethren** and the reason that he did, is that the church is no stronger than its spiritual leadership!

In order to keep it that way we must guard against this particular deadly sin.

You see, even though church harmony is a powerful thing - even though it is a source of strength - **it is also a fragile thing - and as such it must be protected and guarded.** This is what Paul is saying in Ephesians 4:2-3. We must, *"Make EVERY EFFORT to keep the unity of the Spirit through the bond of peace."* I'm using the word **"MUST"** so frequently to help you realize that it is IMPERATIVE that we UNDERSTAND this fact and then strive to steer clear of this particular <u>**sin - because it is a sin that the devil has used countless times to damage and even destroy Christian unity**</u>.

"Make every effort to keep the unity of the Spirit through the bond of peace."
Ephesians 4:2-3

Now, I think the first step in this UNDERSTANDING is an awareness of what it is that MOTIVATES us to sow dissension. There are several but I want to mention only two.

CREEPING BLACK MOLD

1. **The first and one of the main motivators of those who sow dissension is <u>SELFISHNESS</u>.**

    You see, many people come into a church expecting the congregation to feed them - to entertain them - to serve them - to meet their needs. And when a church doesn't meet their needs, or suit their tastes - they complain and gossip and slander - and in this way, they selfishly wreak havoc in a congregation.

    Philip Yancey once illustrated the destructive effects of self-contentedness in his description of the behavior of sea gulls. He writes, **"It's easy to see why people like the seagull."**

    "I've sat overlooking a craggy harbor and watched one. He exults in his freedom. He thrusts his wings backward with powerful strokes, climbing higher and higher until he's above all the other gulls, then he coasts downward in majestic loops and circles. He constantly performs, as if he knows a movie camera is trained on him, recording. In a FLOCK, though, the seagull is a different bird. His majesty and dignity melt into a sordid mass of in-fighting and cruelty.

    Watch that same gull as he dive-bombs into a group of gulls, provoking a flurry of scattered feathers and angry squawks to steal a tiny morsel of meat. The concepts of sharing and manners do not exist among gulls. They are so fiercely

Chapter Eight

competitive and jealous that if you tie a red ribbon around the leg of one gull, making him stand out, you sentence him to execution. The others in the flock will furiously attack him with claws and beaks, hammering through feathers and flesh to draw blood. They'll continue until he lies flattened in a bloody heap."

Unfortunately this is an accurate picture of many churches - where one or more forms of selfishness has led to infighting so fierce that the church eventually becomes lifeless!!

Well, relationships in a church must be the other way around - not self-centered but OTHER-CENTERED. As Paul Powell writes, "The purpose of the church is not just mutual enjoyment, but also mutual enrichment for spiritual development."

- In a biological family we work to help each other grow to emotional and physical maturity. In a healthy family that is our focus - helping each other.

- **And the same is true in a healthy spiritual family. It's a place where we work to help not ourselves - but each other.** We see this reflected in the New Testament's numerous "one another's" commands. I counted 33 such commands. Here's a sampling.

CREEPING BLACK MOLD

In God's Word we are commanded to:

"Love one another"
(John 13:34-35)
"Depend on one another"
(Romans 12:5)

"Honor one another"
(Romans 12:10)

"Rejoice and weep with one another"
(Romans 12:15)

"Admonish one another"
(Romans 15:14)

"Serve one another"
(Galatians 5:13)

"Forgive one another"
(Ephesians 4:32)

"Encourage one another"
(I Thessalonians 5:11)

"Bear one another's burdens"
(Galatians 6:2)

"Confess your 'faults' one to another"
(James 5:16a)

"Pray one for another"
(James 5:16b)

Chapter Eight

...and so on. By reading the New Testament it becomes obvious that God intends the church to be a **SELF-LESS place. When congregations realize that, they enjoy a truly BLESSED fellowship. But when Christians are SELF-CENTERED - so often dissension is the result.**

2. **A second motivator of those who spread dissension is unrealistic EXPECTATIONS.**

This may surprise you but many people expect a church to be full of people who are easy to be with and fun to fellowship with and when that doesn't happen they do one of two things.

- ❖ Either they leave and continue their foolish search for the perfect church, or

- ❖ They attack the imperfection they find in others with gossip or slander or grumbling and complaining.

By the way folks this perception is foolish because <u>**there is no such thing as a perfect church. In fact, the truth is, by its very nature a church will be full of imperfect people - people who can be hard to get along with**</u>.

I worked at a well known shoe store for a time and we had in the back of the store a rack of shoes that was known as the "hash" rack or better known as the **"as is" rack**. There the

CREEPING BLACK MOLD

shopper would know that the inventory on this particular rack was always "**slightly irregular**." You have to shop carefully on this rack because it's expected that you'll find some flaws, i.e., a stain that won't come out...a zipper that won't zip...or a strap is missing. THERE WILL be a problem. Every once in a while you might find some great deals; but, there's a fundamental rule when it comes to purchasing the ultra-low-priced items on this rack, there are no returns...no refunds...no exchanges. If you're looking for that perfect garment, you should shop elsewhere. If you purchase clothes from this rack you take them "**as is**."

Think of it this way------anyone who enters churches looking for perfection, they are shopping on the wrong rack. We've entered the wrong aisle - because the church, **like this fallen world of ours, is full of imperfect people**. As Romans 3:23 says, *"All have sinned and fallen short of the glory of God."*

But **so often Christians do not have this level of maturity -** they expect perfection in the church and this expectation motivates them to sow dissension. In his book **Life Together**, Dietrich Bonhoeffer refers to this when he says, *"Those who love the DREAM of a Christian community more than the Christian community itself become destroyers of that Christian community even though their personal intentions may be ever so honest, earnest, and sacrificial."*

Alright, let's summarize what we've learned so far. The two of the main motivations behind YIELDING to the

Chapter Eight

temptation to sow dissension, are <u>SELF-CENTEREDNESS</u> and <u>UNREALISTIC EXPECTATIONS</u>.

Now, let's examine this deadly sin from the opposite perspective by seeking an answer to this question: What is our motivation to STEER CLEAR of this sin? **What is it that should compel us to PRESERVE church unity and harmony?** Listen closely and be sure to fill in the blanks, for some day you may be able to help out a brother or sister in a church that is going through this very situation:

1. The first thing is that God **COMMANDS** us to strive for Healthy **COMMUNITY**.

    And - that should be all the motivation we require! The fact that God commands it, we should do it!

    "HE DOES?" Well, turn to Matthew 22:37-40. Did you find here that it is God's will that we embrace a healthy relationship with Him and also with our fellow man? In fact, the truth is, these TWO relational commands are really ONE. They are linked - in that you can't fully obey one without fully obeying the other. In I John 4:20 we find that these two greatest commands - these commands that Jesus said are to be foremost as we go about our lives - they are interlinked. We can't love God and not love each other. We can't love God and at the same time do things that damage our unity as a community of believers.

CREEPING BLACK MOLD

And - in our struggle with this **particular deadly sin** we need to understand that the PRIORITY of this command shows us that relational health - is **VERY important to God**.

We see this reflected throughout His written Word. In fact, the New Testament gives more attention to **UNITY** of believers than it does to either **Heaven or Hell.** For example, Ephesians 4:29 says, *"Let no corrupt communication proceed out of your mouth, but that which is good to the use of edifying, that it may minister grace unto the hearers."* In other words it says, **"Build up or shut up."** If what you are saying doesn't add to congregational health, don't say it.

Then verse 30 says that when we ignore this command - **When we damage congregational health with our words and actions we, "...grieve the Holy Spirit of God."** So, like any earthly parent, our Heavenly Father grieves when His kids fight among themselves.

And if you doubt this - then turn with me to the **Gospel of John chapter 17:20-21**. Knowing that the end was near, Jesus prayed one final time for His followers. And He prayed **not for their success, their safety, their happiness, not even for their doctrinal correctness, No, Jesus' FINAL prayer was for their - and OUR - unity**. Foremost in our Savior's mind as He faced the cross was His desire that His fol-

Chapter Eight

lowers would obey God's command down through the ages and enjoy healthy, love-filled community. Think of it this way. **Relational health in the church - UNITY in a local body of believers - is the SOUL of its fellowship. Destroy it with dissension and you will rip the HEART out of Christ's body.**

Now, don't misunderstand me, I'm not saying that God wants unity at all costs. He doesn't want us to ignore disputes over the essential beliefs and doctrines of our faith, if that's what it takes to make everyone happy. NO - NO! Genuine unity would not be possible under those conditions. Our shared convictions that Jesus is God's only Son - and the only way to have eternal life - that the Bible is God's infallible Word - shared essential beliefs like these are the SOURCE of our unity. They are the foundation of congregational health. But what I AM saying is this - **whenever we act UNLOVING. Whenever we GOSSIP or SLANDER or COMPLAIN and GRUMBLE about non-essential things - whenever we carelessly, selfishly, DAMAGE congregational unity and health, we are working contrary to the will - and the nature of GOD**. Whenever we act like the devil and sow dissension we are working for the enemy. Knowing **that** should motivate us to steer clear of this deadly sin.

2. **A second motivation for us to do this is the basic truth that we all <u>NEED</u> community.**

CREEPING BLACK MOLD

Folks, we can't BE Christians on our own. We need each other! A gentleman and he was a gentle man, from northern Michigan, many years ago, became a member of our church and a faithful servant until his home going to Heaven. While he was planning to move to our city, he stopped to eat breakfast at a diner and saw GRITS on the menu. He'd never eaten - or even SEEN grits before, so he asked the waitress, *"What exactly is a grit?"* and one of our members, who was the waitress, gave a classic response, *"Honey, grits don't come by themselves."* And, as a connoisseur of grits, I would say she was right. Grits don't exist in isolation. No grit is an island; every grit is a part of the whole.

Well, the same is true of Christians. We don't come by ourselves. When we acknowledge God as our Father, every other Christian <u>instantly</u> becomes our brother or sister. And that's one of the wonderful things about our faith. **It meets our inborn need for deep fellowship with others.** We do indeed NEED community. We need healthy relationships with others. We're empty otherwise. As Detrick Bonhoeffer said, ***"Whoever cannot stand being IN COMMUNITY should beware of BEING ALONE."*** He's right, because we were created to draw life and nourishment from one

Chapter Eight

another the same way roots of an oak tree draw life from the soil.

Harvard University did a study in which they tracked 7,000 people over nine years. Their researchers found that the most isolated people were three times more likely to die than those with strong relational connections.

3. **The Third reason to compel us to preserve church unity and harmony is that the <u>UNSAVED</u> will be <u>ATTRACTED</u> to healthy <u>BIBLE BELIEVING CHURCHES</u>!**

You see, because of our inborn need for FELLOWSHIP, non-believers are naturally drawn to healthy relationships. A church with a **Sweet, Sweet Spirit** draws people like a moth is drawn to a flame.

This desire is especially strong these days because our society has become so disconnected. Why do you think that there is so much emphasis on sports? Why not become the drawing flame to those that are searching for closeness with each other?

Think of it! Instead of face-to-face discussions <u>we rely on e-mail</u>.

CREEPING BLACK MOLD

Plus, our work days are so long we rarely even speak to our neighbors. When we do finally get home we push the button on the garage door remote and drive in. Then we close it behind us without having to do much more than wave at anyone nearby.

Well, this lifestyle of isolation leaves a void that all people long to fill. And it is time again that churches like ours need to realize that filling this void can provide them, the **lost and unchurched**, a chance to share the gospel. We need to remember that the first step in evangelism is often just to give our non-believing neighbors a taste of authentic community - by inviting them to a Youth Choir concert or a children's choir musical or a church picnic or a VBS family fun night or to play on the church softball team and they - **WE** - are correct in this way of thinking because healthy community fosters belief. People naturally want to be around Christians who act **loving to one another**!

How can we accomplish this? Well, why not on Sundays have an agreement that there will be no criticism in the house and keep to this agreement? There are no fights or quarreling in the home on the Lord's Day. The most striking result, I believe, is that the children's friends end up spending Sundays at their home. They like being in a place where, instead of dissension, there is love. It works the same way in a church family. So, unity

Chapter Eight

fosters belief, but unfortunately the **REVERSE** is also true. Disunity fosters disbelief.

When we sow dissension - when we act unloving toward each other - it distorts our message of love and drives the lost away from Christ.

I read this story the other day and it goes like this: "A little church in a French village once had a beautiful life-size statue of Jesus with his hands outstretched in its courtyard. During WWII a bomb struck too close to the statue and it was shattered - broken into dozens of pieces. After the war the citizens of the village decided to find the pieces of their beloved statue and reconstruct it. Patiently they gathered the broken pieces and reassembled it. At first, they felt good about this because they found that even the cracks - even the scars on the body - added to its beauty. But soon they discovered a problem. You see, they were unable to find the **HANDS** of the statue. They had apparently been blown into nothingness. One church member lamented, *"A Christ without hands is no Christ at all. Hands with scars, yes, but what's a Lord without hands? We need a new statue."*

Then someone else came along with another idea and it prevailed. A brass plaque was added to the base of the statue which read, *"I have no hands,*

CREEPING BLACK MOLD

but your hands." **Years later someone saw the inscription and wrote these familiar lines:**

"Christ has not hands but our hands to do His work today;

He has no feet but our feet to lead men in His way.

He has no tongue but our tongues, to tell men how He died.

"I have no hands, but your hands."

He has no help but our help, to bring men to His side.

We are the only Bible, the careless world will read.

We are the sinner's gospel; we are the scoffer's creed;

We are the Lord's last message, written indeed in word.

We really are His hands."

Ours is the flesh He is now using to accomplish His will. And because it is, we must understand that we are to have happening in our lives individually and in our life collectively as a church, the same attitudes, the same

Chapter Eight

concern, the same involvement, the same mission in life - which Jesus had when He was here in the days of His flesh. So, if we are functioning as a **HEALTHY** body we will always follow the will of **CHRIST**. We'll always **DO WHAT JESUS WOULD DO**. We'll always relate to one another and to the lost world around us in the same way Jesus would.

Well, what does the world around us think when we, the body of Christ, do not let him rule? What does our community think **when we fail to love one another as He commands**?

In Philip Yancey's book, ***Disappointment with God***, Carolyn Martin has cerebral palsy, and it is the peculiar tragedy of her condition that it's outward signs - - - drooling, floppy arm movements, inarticulate speech, a bobbing head - cause people who meet her to wonder if she is retarded. Actually, her mind is the one part of her that works perfectly; it is muscular control that she lacks. Carolyn lived for fifteen years in a home for the mentally retarded, because the state had no other place for her. Her closest friends were people like Larry, who tore all his clothes off and ate the institution's houseplants, and Arelene, who only knew three sentences and called everyone "*Mama*."

Carolyn determined to escape from the home and to find a meaningful place for herself in the outside

CREEPING BLACK MOLD

world. Eventually, she did manage to move out and establish a home of her own. There, the simplest chores posed an overwhelming challenge. It took her three months to learn to brew a pot of tea and pour it into cups without scalding herself. But Carolyn mastered that feat and many others. She enrolled in high school, graduated, then signed up for community college. Everyone on campus knew Carolyn as *"the disabled person."* They would see her sitting in a wheelchair, hunched over, painstakingly typing out notes on a device called a Canon Communicator. Few felt comfortable talking with her; they could not follow her jumbled sounds. But Carolyn persevered, stretching out a two year Associate of Arts degree program over seven years. Next, she enrolled in a Lutheran college to study the Bible. After two years there, she was asked to speak to her fellow students in chapel. Carolyn worked many hours on her address. She typed out the final draft - - - at her average speed of forty-five minutes per page - - - and asked her friend Josee to read it for her. Josee had a strong, clear voice. On the day of the chapel service, Carolyn sat slumped in her wheelchair on the left side of the platform. At times her arms jerked uncontrollably, her head lolled to one side...so that it almost touched her shoulder, and a stream of saliva sometimes ran down her blouse.

Beside her stood Josee, who read the mature and graceful prose Carolyn had composed, centered

Chapter Eight

on this Bible text: *"...but we have this treasure in jars of clay to show that this all surpassing power is from God but not from us."* For the first time, some students saw Carolyn as a complete human being, like themselves. Before then, her mind, a very good mind, had always been inhibited by a *"disobedient"* body, and difficulties with speech had masked her intelligence. But hearing her address read aloud as they looked at her on stage, the students could see past the body in a wheelchair and imagine a whole person. Carolyn was a perfect mind locked inside a spastic, uncontrolled body, and vocal cords that failed at every second syllable.

When I read this story, the New Testament image of Christ as head of the body takes on new meaning. So often I think that we - the local church - disobey Christ in the same unruly way in which Carolyn's body disobeyed her.

When we fail to love one another as He loved us - when we sow dissension - then like Carolyn's body, we obscure rather than convey the message of God's love. This repels people from God - in much the same way that people avoided Carolyn because of her body's disobedient actions.

When we fight among ourselves we do not draw people to Jesus' love **because they do not recognize Him in us**.

CREEPING BLACK MOLD

In which way are we guilty?

Are we truly in love with each other as Christ loved us?

Or

Are we guilty of sowing discord among God's church?

Chapter Eight

THOUGHTS:
_____
_____
_____
_____
_____
_____
_____
_____

ACTIONS:
_____
_____
_____
_____
_____
_____
_____
_____

CREEPING BLACK MOLD

CONCLUSION

The book of Proverbs is very practical, especially this sixth chapter, because it concerns the believer's daily walk with God. It is true that it does not contain much doctrine, **but it sure does emphasize the daily practice and walk of the believer**.

One writer describes the book of Proverbs **this** way: *"While other parts of Scripture show us the glory of our high calling, this may instruct in all minuteness of detail how to 'walk worthy of it.'"* Elsewhere, we learn our completeness in Christ and most justly we glory in our high exaltation as **"joint heirs with Christ."** We must see the minuteness of our Christian obligation; that there is not a temper, a look, a word, a movement, the most important action of the day, the smallest relative duty, in which we do not either deface or adorn the image of our Lord, and the profession of His name.

After you finish this book and study, I believe you will see how the believer **"may adorn the doctrine of God our Saviour**

in all things" (Titus 2:10). Even the unsaved recognize this chapter as a manual for conduct, so how much more should it apply to all Christians, who have the wonderful indwelling of the Holy Spirit to help us live the life that will lead others to Christ and other Christians to a closer walk with Him.

Remember that the only way to get rid of "THE CREEPING BLACK MOLD" is to remove the problem and the only way to remove sin in your life is through the blood of Jesus Christ on a daily basis (I John 1:9).

We must remember that the *"heart is deceitful above all things, and desperately wicked"* (Jeremiah 17:9).

It was D. L. Moody that said, *"Looking at the wound of sin will never save anyone. What you must do is look at the remedy."*

Thank God,
Jesus Christ is the remedy!

CREEPING BLACK MOLD

God bless you as you walk closer to your

Saviour and Lord.

(GS)

CREEPING BLACK MOLD

NOTES:

CREEPING BLACK MOLD

NOTES:

CREEPING BLACK MOLD

NOTES:

CREEPING BLACK MOLD

Dr. Gene Schuyler

Author of:

Total Surrender

Give Me An Old Shoe

The Scarlet Thread of Redemption

STUDENT WORKSHEETS

CREEPING BLACK MOLD

"THE CREEPING BLACK MOLD"

CHAPTER ONE

Student Worksheet

The Seven Sins of Proverbs - INTRODUCTION

Stac/hy/botrys char/tarum - It is commonly known as "**toxic _____.**"

I. A _____ Look

II. A _____ Tongue

III. Hands that _____ Innocent Blood

IV. A Heart filled with Wicked _____

V. Feet that are swift in running to _____

VI. False _____

VII. Sowers of _____

What is sin? John tells us in his first epistle that "_____ _____ is sin...."

So, as you can see how horrible are these sins and how we must be careful that they do not invade our lives.....

In the next chapters, we will begin looking at these individually.

APPLICATION:

    How are you going to apply this?

STUDENT WORKSHEETS

"THE CREEPING BLACK MOLD"

CHAPTER TWO

Student Worksheet

Sin #1: "PRIDE" – Proverbs 6:16

Pride is the precursor to virtually all other forms of sin; it is the soil in which all kinds of wickedness germinate and grow (Proverbs 16:18-19; 18:12; 21:4; 29:23).

Is it really the case that pride is the precursor to or perhaps the root of most sin? Yes!

E_____; B_____; S_____ D_____;
H_____; S_____; G_____.

1. **THE PROBLEM WITH PRIDE**

    I. **WHAT PRIDE IS NOT**

        a. Pride is not a _____ self-image
        b. Pride is not _____ for a job well done

    II. **WHAT IS PRIDE?**

        a. An attitude of _____ from God
        b. A spirit of _____ to God
        c. Esteeming ourselves _____ than others

    III. **INDICATORS OF A PROUD PERSON**

        a. A _____ person becomes irritated when corrected for mistakes

CREEPING BLACK MOLD

    b.   A _____ person accepts praise for things over which he or she has no control (i.e. beauty, talents, abilities)

    c.   A proud person has an ungrateful spirit for all that God has done

    d.   A proud person often finds himself in competition with others

IV.   **FIVE THINGS PRIDE WILL DO TO DEVASTATE AND RUIN YOUR LIFE**

    a.   Pride _____ God
    b.   Pride _____ man
    c.   Pride _____ society
    d.   Pride _____ life
    e.   Pride _____ souls
    i.   Pride is the road to _____

        1.   _____ ruin (2 Chronicles 7:14)
        2.   _____ ruin
        3.   _____ ruin
        4.   _____ ruin
        5.   _____ ruin

CONCLUSION:

Jesus Christ is the greatest example ever of humility. We who take the name of Christ need to live as Christ did - _____.

APPLICATION:

    How are you going to apply this?

STUDENT WORKSHEETS

"THE CREEPING BLACK MOLD"

CHAPTER 3

Student Worksheet

Sin #2: "TO TELL THE TRUTH" – Proverbs 6:16

One form of lying could be called, "the S_____ lie."

Then there is lying by F_____.

T_____ can be used to tell a lie.

I. **WHAT IS LYING?**

    A. _____ Idea

    B. _____ Sense

    C. _____ Deception

II. **WHY DO PEOPLE LIE?**

    A.   Out of _____

    B.   To S_____ Responsibility

    C.   To H_____ Someone

    D.   To Get _____

    E.   For the "G_____ Good"

CREEPING BLACK MOLD

III. THE O_____ OF ALL LIARS.

    A.   God W_____ us not to Lie

    B.   Lying is D_____ to God – Prov. 6:16-17; 12:22 (despicable)

    C.   Therefore, He will Punish A_____ Liars

IV. WHAT HAPPENS WHEN WE LIE?

    A.   Well, first off...when we lie WE HURT _____.

    B.   But we also hurt our R_____ WITH OTHER PEOPLE.

    C.   But you know, the WORST damage caused by lying is that it P_____ US AWAY FROM _____.

    D.   How to overcome lying:

        L _____ the truth.
        L _____ the truth.
        L _____ the truth.

APPLICATION:

How are you going to apply this?

STUDENT WORKSHEETS

"THE CREEPING BLACK MOLD"

CHAPTER 4

Student Worksheet

Sin #3: "MURDER" – Proverbs 6:16

The Bible does not prohibit the **DEATH** penalty? Why?

The philosophy behind capital punishment says that if an individual shows that he does not _____ human life he must forfeit his own, so that others will not lose their right to life at his hands.

Another reason God wants us to see **MURDER** as a sin is because each human life is _____ and we see this from the very beginning in the WAY humans were created.

The greatest proof of the extreme value of each and every human life is seen in the fact that God has said that each life is equal in value to that of _____ _____.

But you know, the greatest proof of the extreme value of each and every human life is seen in the fact that God has said that each life is equal in value to that of His only **SON**.

APPLICATION:

    How are you going to apply this?

CREEPING BLACK MOLD

"THE CREEPING BLACK MOLD"

CHAPTER 5

Student Worksheet

Sin #4: "MISCHIEVOUS FEET" – Proverbs 6:16

Feet Swift In Running To Mischief – Someone said "The heart blazes the trail the feet follow." When "wicked imaginations" are formed in the heart, the feet will be quick to carry them out, Isaiah 59:7.

"Feet that be swift in _____ to Mischief" (Proverbs6:18b).

"My son, walk _____ thou in the way with them; _____ _____: [16] for their _____, and make haste to shed blood" (Proverbs 1:15-16).

"Their _____, and they make haste to shed innocent blood: their thoughts are thoughts of iniquity; wasting and destruction are in their paths" (Isaiah 59:7)

"What Kind of Feet God's People Ought to have?"

I.   God's people should have _____ feet (John 13:1-17).

    1.   God's people must learn from His _____ (John 13:4-5).

    2.   God's people must learn from His _____ (John 13:12-17).

II.   God's People Ought to have _____ feet: Bringers of Good News are P___e___i___us and B___a___ti____ (Isaiah 52:7; Romans 10:14-17).

III.   God's people ought to have _____ FEET.

STUDENT WORKSHEETS

God Has Sent People—YOU AND I THAT ARE B_____ A_____ -- with the G_____ News.

"So then _____ cometh by hearing, and _____ by the word of God" (Romans 10:17).

III.   God's people ought to have "_____ _____" (Ephesians 6:15).

IV.   The _____ of Having Our Feet Shod (Ephesians 2:11-12).

Four things that we learn from those two verses:

1.   All _____ Is War.

2.   The War Is Against _____ Evil Powers.

3.   There Is Danger of _____ in This Battle.

4.   God Has Made Provision for Us to _____ and not _____ (Jude, Verse 24).

APPLICATION:

How are you going to apply this?

CREEPING BLACK MOLD

"THE CREEPING BLACK MOLD"

CHAPTER 6

Student Worksheet

Sin #5: "A WICKED HEART" – Proverbs 6:18a

THE HEART OF THE PROBLEM IS THE PROBLEM OF THE HEART

1. The HEART is a POOR STUDENT OF GOD'S WORD - WHAT IT _____ (Proverbs 6:1-6).

2. The HEART is a MASTER OF DISGUISE - WHAT IT _____ (Proverbs 6:7-14).

3. Your HEART is a window into your SOUL - WHAT IT _____ (Proverbs 6:15-20).

4. With all this known to us up to now: what are the lessons we need to learn?

    I. God _____ our HEART (Luke 16:14-15).
    II. We MUST _____ and _____ our HEARTS in order to examine and improve ourselves (2 Corinthians 13:5).
    III. Like _____, we can be people "AFTER GOD'S OWN HEART."

CONCLUSION/APPLICATION:

1. The _____ in heart shall see God (Matthew 5:8).
2. _____ your heart – Life issues from it (Proverbs 4:23).

EXTRA NOTES:

STUDENT WORKSHEETS

"THE CREEPING BLACK MOLD"

CHAPTER 7

Student Worksheet

Sin #6: "BEARING FALSE WITNESS" – Proverbs 6:16

1. A False _____ will use harsh words that only _____ and are meant to _____ and _____ pain.

2. A False _____ brings self-destruction (Proverbs 19:5; 21:28; and Isaiah 54:1; James 3:4-6).

   The _____ and the _____ (James 3:2b-3).
   The _____ and the _____ (James 3:4).

   Men and women lie because they are more concerned with the self than anything else. Why (John 12:43)?
   _____
   _____
   _____

   _____ is a powerful angelic being that broadcasts—all over the Earth—a spirit of _____, which includes lying and deception (Ephesians 2:2). It is _____ who tempts all humans to lie.

   YOUR REPUTATION IS A _____ POSSESSION (Proverbs 22:1).

   ➤ Your _____ Determines The Level Of

CREEPING BLACK MOLD

_____ You Receive - No one puts much confidence in a person who is dishonest, deceptive, or otherwise living his life in a sinful, shameful manner. You respect people about whom you never hear a negative remark. Jesus was such a man - Luke 2:52.

➢ Your own reputation is valuable. Therefore, _____ it with your very life. You cannot be _____ for what others do with your reputation, but you are _____ for what you do with theirs.

YOUR REPUTATION CAN BE _____ PUBLICLY.

APPLICATION:

How are you going to apply this?

STUDENT WORKSHEETS

"THE CREEPING BLACK MOLD"

CHAPTER 8

Student Worksheet

Sin #7: "THE DANGER OF SOWING DISCORD!" – Proverbs 6:16

Now, I think the first step in this UNDERSTANDING, is an awareness of what it is that MOTIVATES us to sow dissension. There are several but I want to mention only two.

1. The first and one of the main motivators of those who sow dissension is _____.

2. A second motivator of those who spread dissension is unrealistic _____.

Now, let's examine this deadly sin from the opposite perspective by seeking an answer to this question: What is our motivation to STEER CLEAR of this sin? What is it that should compel us to PRESERVE church unity and harmony?

1. The first thing is that God _____ us to strive for healthy _____.

2. A second motivation for us to do this is the basic truth that we all _____ community.

3. The Third reason to compel us to preserve church unity and harmony is that the _____ will be _____ to healthy _____.

CREEPING BLACK MOLD

RECAP

1. _____
2. A LYING _____
3. _____
4. FEET RUNNING TO _____
5. A HEART WITH WICKED _____
6. _____ WITNESS
7. _____ OF DISCORD

What have I _____?

APPLICATION:

How are you going to apply this?

www.ingramcontent.com/pod-product-compliance
Lightning Source LLC
LaVergne TN
LVHW010316070426
835507LV00026B/3422